TRUST DOCTRINES IN CHURCH CONTROVERSIES

TRUST DOCTRINES IN CHURCH CONTROVERSIES

by
DALLIN H. OAKS

MERCER

ISBN 0-86554-XXX-X

KF
740
.O2
1984

TRUST DOCTRINES IN CHURCH CONTROVERSIES
COPYRIGHT ©1984 BY
MERCER UNIVERSITY PRESS, MACON GA 31207
ALL RIGHTS RESERVED
PRINTED IN THE UNITED STATES OF AMERICA

ALL BOOKS PUBLISHED BY MERCER UNIVERSITY PRESS
ARE PRODUCED ON ACID-FREE PAPER THAT EXCEEDS
THE MINIMUM STANDARDS SET BY THE NATIONAL
HISTORICAL PUBLICATIONS AND RECORDS COMMISSION.

LIBRARY OF CONGRESS CATALOGING IN PUBLICATION DATA

Oaks, Dallin H.
    Trust doctrines in church controversies.

    1. Church property—United States. 2. Religious trusts—United States. 3. Corporations, Religious—United States. 4. Church property—California. 5. Religious trusts—California. 6. Corporations, Religious—California.   I. Title.
KF4868.C40197   1984   346.73'064   83-25058
ISBN 0-86554-104-3 (alk. paper)   347.30664

CONTENTS

I. INTRODUCTION 1

II. RELIGOUS TRUSTS AND CORPORATIONS UNDER
    THE COMMON LAW OF ENGLAND............................ 11
    A. The Regulatory Authority of Chancery and
       the Attorney General as a Precedent
       for American Common Law................................ 13
       1. The enforcement authority of the Crown,
          chancellor, and attorney general........................ 14
       2. The statutory enforcement authority
          of commissioners... 20
       3. The enforcement authority of visitors 21
    B. Church Property Disputes................................. 25

III. THE COMMON LAW OF RELIGIOUS TRUSTS AND
    CORPORATIONS IN THE UNITED STATES 31
    A. Church Property Disputes................................. 33
    B. Judicial and Attorney General Supervisory
       Authority over Religious Charitable Trusts
       and Corporations 42
       1. The validity of charitable trusts 43
       2. The enforcement of charitable trusts.................. 44
       3. The charitable corporation 55
          a. Visitorial powers..................................... 55
          b. Quo warranto.. 59

     c. Enforcement or supervisory authority
        over corporations 61
    4. Charitable trusts and
       corporations compared 65

IV. STATE LEGISLATION FOR THE SUPERVISION OF
     CHARITABLE TRUSTS AND CORPORATIONS.................. 73

V. CALIFORNIA CASES AND STATUTES............................ 79

VI. CONSTITUTIONAL CONSIDERATIONS
     AND CONCLUSION 99
    A. Regulatory Authority 99
      1. Free exercise 101
      2. Establishment 104
      3. Compelling state interest and
        alternate means tests.................................... 107
    B. Church Property Disputes.................................. 113
      1. Three theories of the
        neutral-principles approach........................... 117
        a. Nondetermination of religious law
          or polity.. 117
        b. Neutrality in religious
          decisionmaking....................................... 118
        c. Deference to church
          decisionmakers 120
      2. Future application of the
        neutral-principles approach........................... 121

FOREWORD

MERCER STUDIES IN LAW AND RELIGION:
AMERICAN LEGAL CULTURE AND COUNTERCULTURE

The publication of a new series of monographs on law and religion by the Center for Constitutional Studies at Mercer University is at once a contribution to American culture and a manifestation of a growing counterculture. It is a contribution to our culture in that it seeks to probe in a scholarly fashion the deepest roots of the American experience regarding the appropriate relationship between law and religion. It is countercultural at least in the sense that it attempts to juxtapose two disciplines that many, if not most, of our contemporaries regard as neatly divided categories having little to do with one another. Each of these assertions merits further comment, for they will serve as guiding principles for the selection of subsequent themes to be included in this series of monographs.

It must be stated at the outset that the Mercer Studies in Law and Religion should not be defined negatively as a series of tracts against a particular view or set of views concerning law and religion. Rather, these studies will serve the positive function of exploring particular instances that have shaped the relationship between law and religion in this country. Although monographs in the Mercer Studies may occasionally include an exploration of relevant English legal history, the primary focus will be on the American experience. For example, the inaugural volume in the series displays the careful and thorough research of Justice Dallin H. Oaks concerning the English common law on trusts and its application to the resolution of church controversies on both sides of the Atlantic. On the other hand, a systematic exploration of the origins of the western legal tradition, such as that set forth by Professor Harold J. Berman in his masterful volume, *Law and Revolution* (Harvard University Press, 1983), lies beyond the scope of this series. By bringing to the attention of a wider audience significant essays on the general theme of the series, the Mercer Studies will attempt to contribute to the general understanding of American legal culture as it has been shaped by religious experience and insight.

On the other hand, the Mercer Studies will be counter-cultural in the sense that the intention of the series is not to confirm too facile a separation of law and religion. According to the received wisdom, the primary source of constitutionalism and other fundamental legal concepts and institutions is to be sought in the secularizing and often frankly anti-religious tendency of certain philosophers of the European Enlightenment of the eighteenth century, who sought to dichotomize and polarize law and religion. By contrast, the Mercer Studies on Law and Religion will attempt neither to claim too much for religion or for law, nor to deny a legitimate measure of autonomy for each, but to demonstrate that the relationship between law and religion has not always been antithetical or hostile, and to explore on occasion the religious roots of legal concepts and institutions (generally regarded as thoroughly secular in origin) as well as ways in which secular legal developments have influenced religious understanding. The publication of the Mercer Studies in Law and Religion will, in general, be guided by the major theme of Professor Harold J.

Berman's seminal volume, *The Interaction of Law and Religion*. In this essay Berman wrote:

> Law and religion are two different but interrelated aspects, two dimensions of social experience—in all societies, but especially in Western society today. Despite the tensions between them, one cannot flourish without the other. Law without . . . religion degenerates into a mechanical legalism. Religion without . . . law loses its social effectiveness.[1]

If this view does not reflect the mainstream of American legal philosophy, the Mercer Studies in Law and Religion will, to some extent, be swimming against the current.

SCHOLARSHIP AND PRACTICALITY

This series of monographs is well inaugurated by Dallin Oaks' study on the use of the law of charitable trusts in the resolution of controversies among members of a religious body or between a religious body and the government. This essay blends careful scholarship with practical wisdom. Oaks is one of those rare individuals equally at home in the groves of academe (where he is widely recognized as a preeminent legal scholar) and in the corridors of public power (where he now serves as a Justice of the Utah Supreme Court). During his two decades of service at the University of Chicago Law School and at Brigham Young University, he earned the reputation of being a diligent scholar and professor as well as a fair and able President of the largest religiously-affiliated university in this country. Oaks served as President of the American Association of Presidents of Independent Colleges and Universities, and in that capacity he frequently and skillfully advocated before Congress the need for preserving intact the autonomy and integrity of America's independent institutions of higher education. Reflecting the blend of scholarship and practicality manifested in the career of the author, this monograph discloses an extraordinary depth of intelligence and a direct relevance to public policy matters. Each of these features of Oaks' monograph merits further comment.

---

[1] *The Interaction of Law and Religion* (Nashville: Abingdon Press, 1974) 11.

First, Oaks' study is a model of careful and thorough scholarship. It subjects to critical examination assumptions taken for granted before the publication of his views in the *Brigham Young University Law Review* in 1981. Oaks' exhaustive review of all relevant judicial authorities leads ineluctably to a repudiation of claims that the common law provides a basis for broad supervisory powers of state attorneys general over religious charities. The widespread notion that such supervisory jurisdiction was conferred by statute is likewise shown to be but a commonly-held mistake. In a single paragraph deftly summarizing the groundbreaking conclusions of his research, Oaks shows that the assertion of far-reaching authority over churches made by the California Attorney General is wholly unsupported by American and English legal history:

> California's public trust doctrine is descended not from the common law of judicial and attorney general enforcement authority over charitable trusts, but from a misapplication of the implied trust doctrine that the English and American courts evolved as a tool for resolving church property disputes. Born a naked legal fiction, the doctrine of implied trust had a robust role in church property disputes in this country for about a century but has now been consigned to oblivion as a dispute-settlement mechanism by 1969 and 1979 United States Supreme Court decisions holding it unconstitutional. With that illegitimate ancestry, California's unique court decisions and legislative enactments using the implied trust doctrine to justify judicial and attorney general supervision of religious charities are at least seriously suspect on the same grounds. The California Court of Appeal decisions on church property disputes are taking these constitutional doubts seriously, and the Legislature has responded to the excesses of the attorney general by rescinding the legislative basis for the public trust doctrine. (p. 101)

This tightly written paragraph summarizes months of painstaking research; each sentence encapsulates a closely-reasoned argument leading clearly to the conclusions that Oaks expresses gracefully. In sum, Oaks is a legal scholar *par excellence*.

FROM THEORY TO PRACTICE:
"THE WORLDWIDE CHURCH OF GOD" CASE

Second, Oaks' study can be pragmatically useful in shaping public policy affecting the relationship between church and state in the United States. The Canadian philosopher and theologian, Bernard Lonergan, has stated well the connection between clear thinking and correct judgment and decisions: "to be practical is to do the intelligent thing, and to be impractical is to keep blundering about."[2] The truism that ideas generally have consequences takes nothing from Oaks' achievement as a scholar. On the contrary, it is often the hallmark of true scholars that their ideas shape subsequent events. In the present instance, Oaks' essay helped to influence the climate of ideas in California relating to state regulatory authority over religious bodies. As I have already suggested, the ideas that held sway, at least in some circles of power in California before the appearance of Oaks' article, had disastrous consequences for the freedom of churches not only in that state but also in other jurisdictions that tend to follow the lead of large, populous states.

In early 1979, the State of California commenced extraordinary proceedings in Los Angeles against the Pasadena-based Worldwide Church of God, run by Herbert Armstrong, Sr. The potential threat for religious freedom of all churches posed by the claims of the California Attorney General to supervisory power over the Worldwide Church of God should have been apparent to the judiciary from the outset of that case. Until well after the State legislature repealed the statutory authority for regulatory power over churces, however, the judges involved in the case remained supine in the face of extravagant claims of State authority over churches. For example, Hillel Chodos, the Special Deputy Attorney General representing the State of California in the case, urged the trial court to put the church into receivership on the ground that:

> There are no privileges, constitutional or otherwise of a charitable foundation against intervention by the Attorney General. . . .
>
> Every other party who comes before this court has some claim to its own property and has some right to resist intervention by the Court. but for 700 years, Your Honor, it has been the law in England and America that charitable funds are public funds. They are per-

---

[2] *Insight: A Study of Human Understanding* (New York: Philosopher's Library, 1957) xiii-xiv.

petually in the custody of the court. The court is the ultimate cus-
todian of all church funds, just as the Attorney General has always
been charged with the power and duty to investigate allegations of
misuse or even suspicions of misuse. . . .

Your Honor has the power and the discretion to safeguard and
preserve those assets and the duty to do so. But the church, as a charitable trust, has no interest to protect here. It has no client. It is the
court's funds, and the court may remove and replace the substitute
trustees at its pleasure.

Perhaps after the *Worldwide Church of God* case, no judge would grant
to a state the relief sought by the State of California, but it is sobering
to note that a jurisdiction renowned for its judiciary actually allowed
the government to take over and manage a church. If it is unlikely
that such an improbable result will recur again soon, that is in no
small measure due to the publication of Oaks' refutation of the spu-
rious legal history presented to the courts in the *Worldwide Church of
God* case.

The magnitude of the governmental assault on religious freedom represented by the Attorney General's position in that case was
put in bold relief in an article by Morton B. Jackson, who framed that
position in nine theses:

1. The State controls and supervises the use of all church assets and
may punish those who attempt to evade state-mandated
restrictions.

2. The State can appropriate church funds to pay the salaries and
expenses of the State's supervisors and investigators.

3. The State may remove church leaders if it has the slightest suspicion that they are not following State dictates.

4. Churches have no right to the Due Process of Law guaranteed by
the United States Constitution.

5. Churches have no right to defend themselves against the State,
nor to retain counsel of their own choosing.

6. The State determines how churches are to be governed.

7. The State can examine and physically take all church records regardless of the chilling effect this might have on membership and
participation.

8. Church members have no right to protect their church or direct
ht how ow their contributions should be spent.

9. The people of the State of California own and control all property of churches incorporated in California, even if no California citizen has ever contributed to the church.[3]

When stated so starkly, the position of the Attorney General of California appears plainly unconstitutional. Yet the eminent constitutional scholar, Professor Laurence H. Tribe, was unsuccessful in his efforts to persuade the United States Supreme Court to grant review of the action of the California courts siding with the Attorney General, despite an unassailable argument by Tribe in his petition for a writ of certiorari:

> It is unconstitutional for the State to assert supervisory authority over the churches on the ground that they are charitable entities and therefore owned by the public, because the ownership assertion is comprehensible *only* on the State's own explicit premise that a charitable organization such as "the Worldwide Church of God derives its position, its existence, from the State of California," and because acceptance of the ownership assertion would "sanction a naked confiscation of private property without just compensation."

Although the Supreme Court declined to review the case, fortunately for the preservation of religious freedom, the California legislature in 1980 repealed the statute relied upon by Attorney General (now Governor) George Deukmejian, and the case against the Worldwide Church of God was dismissed. It would be anachronistic to credit Oaks' article with causing the repeal of the offending statue, but it would not be excessive to assert that if this issue arises again in California or elsewhere, the advocates of state control of a church on a public trust theory will have to reckon with the formidable scholarship of Dallin Oaks that vitiates the public trust theory completely. Oaks' monograph, as well as the thoughtful contributions on this theme by several other leading authorities on church-state matters such as Sharon L. Worthing, Dean M. Kelley, and Charles M. Whelan, S. J.,[4] will stand as a source of practical wisdom to guide attorneys

---

[3] Morton B. Jackson, "Socialized Religion: California's Public Trust Theory," 16 *Valparaiso Univ. L. Rev.* 185 (1981):187-96.

[4] See, for example, Sharon L. Worthing, "The State Takes Over a Church," *Annals* 446 (1979):136ff; Dean M. Kelley, "A Church in Receiv-

general, governors, members of state legislatures and other public policymakers in future determinations of the limits of state supervisory authority over the administration and expenditure of church funds. Because Oaks' study is so carefully researched and so skillfully written, it deserves dissemination to a wider audience than that reached by the original version of the article that appeared in the *Brigham Young University Law Review*. For this reason, it is a distinct honor for the Center for Constitutional Studies at Mercer University to commence its series of monographs on law and religion with a study that will undoubtedly shape the future of the law of church-state relations in this country.

ACKNOWLEDGMENTS

The staff of the *Brigham Young University Law Review* graciously granted permission to reprint copyrighted material that originally appeared in the 1981 volume of that *Review*. The president of Brigham Young University, Jeffrey R. Holland, gave a generous publication subsidy to help inaugurate this series of monographs. My colleagues, Sister Sally Furay, R.C.S.J., Provost of the University of San Diego; Professor William A. Kaplin of the Catholic University of America Law School; and The Reverend Charles M. Whelan, S.J., Professor of Law at Fordham Law School, have agreed to serve as an advisory panel to assist in the selection of subsequent monographs to be published in this series. I am deeply grateful to all of these colleagues and friends for their invaluable assistance in this project.

I am likewise grateful to the Executive Director of the Center for Constitutional Studies at Mercer University, W. Newton Moore, Esq., and to the Director of the Mercer University Press, Dr. Watson E. Mills, whose support for this project has been unflagging.

Edward McGlynn Gaffney, Jr.
James P. Bradley, Professor of Constitutional Law
Loyola Law School, Los Angeles
Editor, Mercer Studies in Law and Religion
October 31, 1983

ership: California's Unique Theory of Church and State," *The Christian Century* 97 (June 18-25, 1980):669ff; and Charles M. Whelan, S.J., "Who Owns the Churches?," in Dean M. Kelley, ed., *Government Intervention in Religious Affairs* (New York: Pilgrim Press, 1981) 57-64.

I

INTRODUCTION*

The last two decades of the twentieth century are likely to involve more frequent legal conflicts between church and state. These conflicts are a result of the general growth in government regulation of private activities, the expanding role of government as provider of social welfare services traditionally provided by churches, the insatiable revenue requirements of government and churches, and the

* Dallin H. Oaks is a Justice of the Utah Supreme Court. This essay was written prior to the author's January 1, 1981, appointment to the Court, while he was immediate past president of Brigham Young University and Professor of Law in its J. Reuben Clark Law School. Dean Rex E. Lee and Professors James H. Backman, W. Cole Durham, Jr., Eugene B. Jacobs, and James E. Sabine of the J. Reuben Clark Law School made helpful suggestions on drafts of parts of this manuscript. Law students Jeanne Bryan Inouye, Kaplin S. Jones, and Ralph Crockett Pond gave valuable research assistance.

increasing secularization of society. In addition, the United States Supreme Court has recently discarded a century-old set of state court precedents governing the settlement of church property disputes by holding that "the First Amendment prohibits civil courts from resolving church property disputes on the basis of religious doctrine and practice."[1] The development of so-called "neutral principles of law"[2] for deciding such controversies will require decades of definitional litigation in the state courts, with constitutional oversight from Washington. The resolution of church-state conflicts will be hampered by uncertainty in the constitutional principles governing the relationship between church and state, including the continuing need for a workable constitutional definition of "religion" usable for purposes of "free exercise" and "establishment."[3]

Doctrines from the law of trusts are likely to have a prominent place in the church controversies of the future, just as in the past. Traditionally, trust doctrines have been employed to resolve disputes between different factions contending for the ownership of church property. More recently, California has used charitable trust doctrines as a basis for exercising judicial and attorney-general enforcement and supervisory authority over the administration of religious charitable trusts and corporations. The use of trust doctrines in both the property dispute and regulatory supervision situations will be examined in this Article. Recent California Court of Appeal decisions provide convenient contemporary illustrations of each of these two types of cases.

---

[1] Jones v. Wolf, 443 U.S. 595, 602 (1979); Presbyterian Church v. Mary E. B. Hull Memorial Presbyterian Church, 393 U.S. 440, 449 (1969). Both cases are discussed in the text accompanying notes 355-56 *infra*.

[2] *See* 443 U.S. at 602-03; 393 U.S. at 449.

[3] *See e.g.*, Kurland, *The Irrelevance of the Constitution: The Religion Clauses of the First Amendment and the Supreme Court*, 24 VILL. L. REV. 3 (1979); Marty, *Of Darters and Schools and Clergymen: The Religion Clauses Worse Confounded*, 1978 SUP CT. REV. 171; Gianella, *Lemon and Tilton: The Bitter and the Sweet of Church-State Entanglement*, 1971 SUP. CT. REV. 147; Oaks, *Religion and Law in the Eighties*, in BELIEF, FAITH AND REASON 109 (J. Howard ed. 1981).

Samoan Congregational Christian Church in the United States v. Samoan Congregational Christian Church of Oceanside[4] involved an attempt by an unincorporated ecclesiastical association of twenty-three Samoan Christian churches to impress a trust upon the assets of one of its constituent churches, a non-profit religious corporation. Acting through its board of of directors, defendant Oceanside Church had discharged its minister and hired a successor. About forty percent of the membership sided with the ousted minister, who appealed his firing to the parent hierarchical association. Acting through its general assembly, the parent disapproved the firing and brought this suit, alleging that the defendant corporation held its properties in trust for the benefit of the parent association and those Oceanside members who remained loyal to that association. The ousted minister and the dissenting minority brought a separate suit, seeking involuntary dissolution of the Oceanside church and distribution of its assets.

Relying on California statutes and cases, the court of appeal concluded that since defendant was a charitable corporation, it held its assets, including those contributed by donors who imposed no trust or other restriction on them, "upon a trust 'to carry out the objects for which the organization was created.' "[5] But the trust was not for the benefit of the plaintiff association. Because "First Amendment values are plainly jeopardized when church property litigation is made to turn on the resolution by civil courts of controversies over religious doctrine and practice,"[6] the type of inquiry necessary to establish plaintiff's trust rights was "constitutionally impermissible."[7] The court could not probe into the "identity of the governing body or bod-

---

[4] 66 Cal. App. 3d 69, 135 Cal. Rptr. 793 (1977).

[5] *Id.* at 74, 135 Cal. Rptr. at 795 (quoting Lynch v. Spilman, 67 Cal. 2d 251, 260, 62 Cal. Rptr. 12, 18 (1967) (citations omitted). Here the court relied on CAL. CORP. CODE § 10206(c) (West 1978), discussed in text accompanying note 254 *infra*, and upon the *Wheelock* and *Pacific Home* cases, discussed in text at notes 238 and 260 *infra*.

[6] Cal. App. 3d at 77, 135 Cal. Rptr. at 796 (quoting Presbyterian Church v. Mary E. B. Hull Memorial Presbyterian Church, 393 U.S. 440, 449 (1969).

[7] *Id.* at 77, 135 Cal. Rptr. at 797.

ies that exercise general authority within a church" or "into the allocation of power within a church organization so as to decide 'where religious law places control over the use of church property.' "[8] Instead, the court of appeal applied "neutral principles of law developed for use in all property disputes" by examining the corporate articles and bylaws.[9] These documents vested control of the Oceanside church and its property in its board of directors, without reference to a trust for the parent association or anyone else. As a result, the court ruled for the defendant corporation, stating that it held its properties as required by the law of nonprofit corporations.

The laws governing the dissolution of nonprofit corporations were applied in the companion case brought by the minority. Here the court of appeal affirmed the trial court's decree dissolving the Oceanside church corporation and, pursuant to the parties' stipulation, directed that forty percent of its assets be transferred to a newly formed religious corporation to serve the minority church membership. That disposition satisfied the attorney general, who, although a party to this litigation, took no sides in the controversy. The attorney general insisted that the assets were impressed with a charitable trust and therefore, under the cy pres doctrine, must be distributed for church purposes and not for private benefit.[10]

Several recent cases illustrate the California attorney general's use of trust doctrines as a basis for supervising and regulating churches. The two most notable involved the Worldwide Church of God and Faith Center, Inc.

Responding to private charges that officers of the Worldwide Church of God were diverting church assets and liquidating church properties at less than market value, attorneys representing the attorney general and a private relator obtained an ex parte order appointing a private attorney as receiver of the church, entered the church's administration building, and took over management of the

---

[8] *Id.* at 77, 135 Cal. Rptr. at 797-98.

[9] *Id.* at 77, 135 Cal. Rptr. at 798.

[10] Fuimaono v. Samoan Congregational Christian Church, 66 Cal. App. 3d 80, 135 Cal. Rptr. 799 (1977). The *Samoan* cases are discussed further in text accompanying notes 289-92 *infra*.

church. The receiver seized records, fired employees, denied access to church officers, stopped payment on outstanding checks, took possession of all assets and records, and monitored and supervised all of the church's business and financial activities. Two and one-half months later, after posting a bond of more than $3 million, the church was allowed to lift the receivership and resume management of its financial affairs. Thereafter, the attorney general amended his complaint to call for, *inter alia*, (1) a formal accounting by designated church officers and corporations of all funds received and disbursed; (2) removal of designated church officers, including Pastor-General Herbert W. Armstrong, as officers and trustees of the church and its affiliated corporations; and (3) an order requiring the church and its affiliated corporations

> to select a board . . . authorized and empowered to oversee and supervise its financial affairs (as distinguished from its ecclesiastical or spiritual affairs), in such manner as to provide reasonable assurance that the charitable trust funds collected and held by such charitable entities will be applied solely to the charitable uses to which they were donated, and will not be diverted or misapplied for the personal benefit of any individual, or for any other improper purposes.[11]

The case then proceeded into contests over the attorney general's attempts at discovery.[12]

---

[11] Second Amended Complaint, People v. Worldwide Church of God, Inc., No. C 267-607 (Cal. Super. Ct. County of Los Angeles July 30, 1979). This controversy has been widely publicized. *E.g.*, Kelley, *A Church in Receivership: California's Unique Theory of Church and State*, CHRISTIAN CENTURY, June 18-25, 1980, at 669; Worthing, *The State Takes Over a Church*, 446 ANNALS, Nov. 1979, at 136; Wiley, *Post-Guyana Hysteria: State of California Occupies Headquarters of the Worldwide Church of God*, LIBERTY, May-June 1979, at 1. The most extensive review is in S. RADER, AGAINST THE GATES OF HELL (1980). *See also* Note, *Government Protection of Church Assets from Fiscal Abuse: The Constitutionality of Attorney General Enforcement under the Religion Clauses of the First Amendment*, 53 S. CAL. L. REV. 1277 (1980).

[12] The trial court directed church officers and corporations to submit to depositions, produce various documents, and answer interrogatories pertaining to the details of receipts and disbursements and other financial transactions, the use of assets of the church and its related entities, and the content of various internal communications among church officials and ministers. This case was dismissed in October 1980 following repeal of the

Younger v. Faith Center, Inc.,[13] an unpublished opinion, is the first appellate decision reviewing the California attorney general's attempt to use statutory authorization and charitable trust theory to regulate religious corporations under the so-called "public trust" theory. To further his investigation of "the business activities" of Faith Center, Inc. and its president and associated entities, the attorney general had petitioned the superior court for enforcement of an administrative subpoena directing the production of fourteen categories of financial, corporate, and personnel documents "to ascertain whether the said nonprofit charitable corporations were complying with the trusts which they have assumed."[14] Finding that the subpoena was properly issued, the trial court had ordered the church official and corporations to comply. In urging the court of appeal to set aside that order, the church contended (1) that its property was not held subject to a public or charitable trust (especially since the pledge slips on which its contributions were received recited that they did not "create a charitable trust") and (2) that enforcement of the order would violate the religion clauses of the first amendment.

The court of appeal approved the subpoenas, reasoning as follows: (1) The properties of nonprofit corporations organized for re-

---

authorizing legislation. *See* text accompanying notes 303-08 *infra*. Relying on abstention principles, the federal court denied an injunction against the receivership order. Worldwide Church of God, Inc. v. California, 623 F.2d 613 (9th Cir. 1980).

[13] Civ. No. 56574 (Cal. Ct. App. Aug. 29, 1980).

[14] *Id*. slip op. at 3. The attorney general relied on CAL. GOV'T CODE § 11180 (West 1978), which authorizes administrative subpoenas, and on CAL. CORP. CODE § 9595 (West 1978) (repealed in 1980, which provided:

A nonprofit corporation which holds property subject to any public or charitable trust is subject at all times to examination by the Attorney General, on behalf of the State, to ascertain the condition of its affairs and to what extent, if at all, it may fail to comply with trusts which it has assumed or may depart from the general purposes for which it is formed.

This section has now been repealed. *See* text accompanying note 294 *infra*.

ligious purposes are "held in trust to carry out the objects for which the organization was created," notwithstanding the pledge documents to the contrary. (2) The attorney general "is empowered to oversee charitable trusts and has primary responsibility for their enforcement." (3) The allegations to the attorney general of "witnesses having personal knowledge of the operations of Faith Center . . . of wrongdoing at Faith Center including among others, allegations of misrepresentation, breach of trust and misappropriation of charitable assets," gave the attorney general a sufficient basis to initiate the subject investigation, since an agency's administrative inquiries can be based "merely on suspicion that the law is being violated, or even just because it wants assurance that it is not." (4) Enforcment of the subpoena would not violate the religion clauses of the first amendment because "the production of documents on a onetime basis" to allow the attorney general to determine whether trust property has been "diverted from its declared purposes" does not subject church organizations to "state control of their financial affairs" or to "interference with their religious beliefs and practices" and therefore "does not result in excessive government entanglement with religion forbidden by the First Amendment."[15]

---

[15] Civ. No. 56574, slip op. at 8, 10-11, 12, 16, 18.

The California attorney general has employed the public trust doctrine with comparable effect in judicial proceedings against the Synanon Foundation. Alleging breach of duty by charitable trustees, the attorney general brought suit against the Foundation for an accounting, damages, and replacement of trustees. The Foundation had been organized in 1958 as a charitable corporation for public education about narcotic addiction, but had amended its articles in 1975 and 1979 to provide that the corporation's primary purpose would be to operate a church to promote the "Synanon religion." In denying defendant's motion for judgment on the pleadings the trial court held (1) that the attorney general had valid common-law and statutory power (under CAL. CORP. CODE §§ 9110-9160 (West Supp. 1981)(effective Jan. 1, 1980)) to bring an action against this corporation because a charitable corporation must use its assets for the purpose expressed in its articles of incorporation; (2) that the state, through its attorney general, can "examine religious organizations in order to ascertain whether they are acting in conformity to their state-chartered nonprofit corporate purposes"; and (3) that such examination does not violate the constitutional rights of churches so long as "the dispute does not require the resolution by civil

In a brief that successfully opposed the Worldwide Church of God's earliest attempt at interlocutory review of some of the discovery orders in the United States Supreme Court, the California attorney general described his public trust theory of jurisdiction over church corporations as follows:

> The courts of California have always held without exception that the secular affairs of church corporations are subject to supervision by the Attorney General and the courts. . . . In general throughout the United States religious purposes are regarded as charitable and trusts for religious purposes are enforced as charitable trusts. . . .
>
> The state attorneys general are charged with such duties of enforcement and supervision because the fulfillment of the purposes of charitable, including religious, organizations is thought to be of general benefit to society as a whole. In that sense, such entities are trustees of their assets for public benefit and hold such assets in trust for the religious or charitable purposes set forth in their governing documents. . . . Any diversion of such funds is a breach of trust. . . . In California and in many other states the attorney general is the only party other than corporate directors or trustees (who in this case are the very persons accused of wrongdoing) who has standing to enforce a charitable trust.[16]

---

courts of controversies over religious doctrine and practice." Synanon Foundation v. California, Civ. Nos. 96566, 96569 (Cal. Super. Ct. Marin County Aug. 8, 1980). These cases were dismissed in October 1980 following repeal of the authorizing legislation. See text accompanying notes 303-08 infra.

[16] Respondent's Brief in Opposition to Petition for Certiorari at 16-17, Worldwide Church of God v. California, 444 U.S. 883 (1979) (citations omitted) (denying cert.). The attorney general's position was described more boldly in the earlier hearings by the attorney for the relators:

> There are no privileges, constitutional or otherwise of a charitable foundation against investigation by the Attorney General. . . .
> . . . But for 700 years, Your Honor, it has been the law in England and America that charitable funds are public funds. They are perpetually in the custody of the court. The court is the ultimate custodian of all church funds, just as the Attorney General has always been charged with the power and duty to investigate allegations of misuse or even suspicions of misuse. . . .
> Your Honor has the power and the discretion to safeguard and preserve those assets and the duty to do so. But the church, as a charitable trust, has no interest to protect here. It has no client. It is the

The use of trust theory as a basis for resolving disputes between factions contending for the ownership of church property has a long history. After a controversial beginning in English common law after the Reformation, the so-called "implied trust" theory was dominant in common-law decisions in our state courts for almost a century until the United States Supreme Court recently discarded it in favor of some alternate like the "neutral-principles" doctrine.[17]

The use of charitable trust theory as a basis for attorney general "enforcement and supervision" of the activities of church trustees or corporations is quite another matter. The attorney general's role as the party responsible for enforcing charitable trusts—a category that includes trusts for the advancement of religion—traces its origin into English law, but the pedigree is not pure. In this area there are significant distinctions between religious trustees and religious corporations, concerns about whether the enforcement doctrine is rooted in judicial power or in the nontransferable prerogatives of the Crown, doubts about the extent to which the English common law in this area was adopted in the American colonies, and a significant overlay of statutory material both in England and in the United States that complicates analysis about whether the judicial or executive authority exercised in this area is common law or statutory.

Finally, the public charitable trust theory the California attorney general articulated in support of his recent enforcement and supervision of religious "trusts" does not lend itself to the "neutral principles" arguably available when courts apply property law concepts to church documents to settle disputes between contending factions. In the resolution of a property dispute the official involvement is limited to a one-time dispute-settlement event, church doctrine does not need to be involved (though it may be), and the attorney general, as representative of the state, is primarily a spectator. On the other

---

court's funds, and the court may remove and replace and substitute trustees at its pleasure.

Appendix, Petition for Certiorari at 170b-172b, Worldwide Church of God, Inc. v. California, 449 U.S. 900 (1980) (denying cert.) *quoted in* Kelley, *supra* note 11, at 671.

[17] *See* discussion in text following note 355 *infra*.

hand, when he uses charitable trust doctrines to enforce or supervise a religious trust or corporation, the attorney general seeks to enforce the terms of a charitable trust against church officials, and is therefore the moving party in an adversary controversy with the church or its leaders. By this means, a government official is involving himself in the administration (albeit property administration) of a church or its constitutent corporations; the involvement is inevitably a continuing one, and there are few "neutral principles" to ameliorate the impact of coercive state action on church administration, ecclesiastical government, and religious practices.

The attorney general's use of charitable trust theory as a justification for the kind of "supervision" of religious organizations described in the *Worldwide Church of God and Faith Center* cases is unprecedented in this country. The first amendment implications of such official action against churches, which have stirred deep concern within the religious community,[18] remain entirely unexplored in the California and United States Supreme Courts, which have never considered such a case on its merits.

This Article will examine the use of common-law charitable trust theory and related statutory enactments in England and the United States, treating both property disputes and regulatory supervision. It will then discuss the implications of such doctrine and practices under the religion clause of the First Amendment of the United States Constitution.

---

[18] *E.g*, authorities cited note 11 *supra*. Dean M. Kelley described the attorney general's action in the *Worldwide Church of God* case as follows:

The most significant aspect of this unprecedented action is the theory advanced by the Attorney General of the State that the income of the church from voluntary contributions is a charitable trust which the State has a duty to protect even against the leaders of the church to which they were given. This innovative doctrine, if accepted by the higher courts, would be of immense moment to all churches and a monumental revision of the present stricture by the U.S. Supreme Court against excessive entanglement by the government in the internal affairs of churches.

Kelley, *Preface*, 446 ANNALS, Nov. 1979, at ix-x.

II

RELIGIOUS TRUSTS AND CORPORATIONS UNDER THE COMMON LAW OF ENGLAND

From earliest times, English Kings were looked upon as the patrons of charitable funds and the guardians of their revenues.[19] Long before the chancellor began to enforce charitable trusts in the 1400s, gifts to corporations for charitable purposes enjoyed some recognition and protection by the courts of law.[20] In this period corporations

---

[19] E. FISCH, D. FREED & E. SCHACHTER, CHARITIES AND CHARITABLE FOUNDATIONS § 19 (1974). This was true at least from the reign of Henry II (1154-89), who decreed that the bishops and abbots held their possession "of the King," so that the Crown was the guardian, patron and founder of their revenues and funds. *Id.* at 12 (quoting Hollis, *Evolution of the Philanthropic Foundation*, 20 EDUC. REC. 575, 581 (1939). *See generally* devises reviewed in Willard, *Illustrations of the Origin of* Cy Pres, 8 HARV. L. REV. 69 (1894).

[20] 4 A. SCOTT, THE LAW OF TRUSTS § 348.2 (3d ed. 1967).

were established by the common law, by "prescription," or by charters from the Crown and Parliament.[21]

Both the charitable trust and the charitable corporation were associated in their origins with religious purposes. "A gift for charitable purposes usually took the form of a gift to a religious corporation," which included a gift to the parson of a parish, who was regarded or formally established as a corporation sole.[22] Concerns that the accumulation of land by or for the benefit of religious bodies was depriving the King and his Lords of the feudal benefits incident to private ownership (an ancient version of modern concerns about removing charitable real estate from the tax rolls) prompted the passage in the 1200s and 1300s of a variety of "mortmain" laws deterring gifts to the church or limiting the amount of property the church could hold.[23] Judging from the terms of this legislation, it had been a very common practice for donors to give property to religious corporations or to individuals in trust for religious persons, orders, or corporations.

By 1601 the charitable trust was so widely used (and abused by variations from the donor's intent, by frauds, and by breaches of trust) that Parliament passed the Statute of Charitable Uses to authorize official "commissioners" to inquire into and take measures to

---

[21] 2 J. KENT, COMMENTARIES ON AMERICAN LAW *276 (14th ed. Gould 1896) [hereinafter cited as KENT'S COMMENTARIES]; Williston, *History of the Law of Business Corporations Before 1800*, 2 HARV. L. REV. 105, 113-14 (1888). The parson of a parish and other religious persons or associations were regarded as corporations by prescription. 4 A. SCOTT, *supra* note 20, § 348.2 at 2780; 1 W. BLACKSTONE, COMMENTARIES *469-74.

[22] 4 A. SCOTT, *supra* note 20, § 348.2, at 2780; 1 W. BLACKSTONE, COMMENTARIES *469-70.

[23] OOSTERHOFF, *The Law of Mortmain: An Historical and Comparative Review*, 27 U. TORONTO L.J. 257, 264-71 (1977); E. FISCH, D. FREED & E. SCHACHTER, *supra* note 19, § 19; 2 W. BLACKSTONE, COMMENTARIES *268-74; R. BRIDGMAN, DUKE'S LAW OF CHARITABLE USES 192-237 (1804); 4 A. SCOTT, *supra* note 20 § 348.2. For example, the earliest legislation forbade religious corporations from holding land, and in 1391 this prohibition was extended to cases where land was conveyed to individuals to the use of religious corporations. *Id.* The predecessor of modern mortmain legislation is the Georgian Statute of Mortmain, 1736, 9 Geo. 2, c.36 (1736).

correct the misuse of property left upon charitable uses.[24] The preamble to this famous statute lists various charitable purposes in force at that time, but its only mention of a religious use is designedly brief, a passing reference to the "repair of churches."[25] After a long period of confusion in England and the United States over the history of the Statute of Charitable Uses, it became clear in the mid-nineteenth century that the Statute had not created charitable trusts, which were valid and enforceable in equity before its passage, but had only established a new and additional means for their enforcement.[26]

A. THE REGULATORY AUTHORITY OF CHANCERY AND THE ATTORNEY GENERAL AS A PRECEDENT FOR AMERICAN COMMON LAW

The modern assertion that the court of chancery and the attorney general had common-law powers to enforce charities can be verified only by a careful examination of the law and practice governing charities in the period that serves as the basis of our own American common law. What was meant by "enforcement" and who was empowered to do it?

Under the English law in force at the time of colonization and the Revolution, there were at least five officials who had some responsibilities in the enforcement of charities, some of whom acted in multiple capacities: (1) the Crown, under its prerogative right as patron

---

[24] 1601, 43 Eliz. 1, c. 4 (1601).

[25] Sir Francis Moore, the draftsman of the statute, explained that gifts for religious uses were purposefully omitted "lest the gifts intended to be employed upon purposes grounded upon charity, might, in change of times (contrary to the minds of the givers) be confiscated into the king's treasury" (because religion is "variable, according to the pleasure of succeeding princes"). E. FISCH, D. FREED & E. SCHACHTER, *supra* note 19, § 272 (quoting DUKE, THE LAW OF CHARITABLE USES 131-32 (1676).

[26] Attorney-General v. Mayor of Dublin, 4 Eng. Rep. 888 (H.L. 1827): Vidal v. Mayor of Philadelphia, 43 U.S. (2 How.) 127 (1844); C. ZOLLMAN, AMERICAN LAW OF CHARITIES §§ 9-26 (1924); Note, *The Enforcement of Charitable Trusts in America: A History of Evolving Social Attitudes*, 54 VA. L. REV. 436, 439 (1968)

of charities; (2) the chancellor, (a) exercising the Crown's prerogative or *parens patriae* right by delegation and (b) exercising the judicial powers of the court of chancery; (3) the attorney general as the representative of the Crown and the moving party to obtain action by the chancellor in one of his two capacities; (4) the commissioners under the Statute of Charitable Uses, and (5), in the case of charitable corporations, the "visitors" or "governors" specified in the conveyance, royal charter, or act of Parliament creating the corporation. Which of these exercised an authority that could serve as a precedent for the American common law of charities?

1. The enforcement authority of the Crown, chancellor, and attorney general

It is well settled that the prerogative power of the Crown "has no place in American jurisprudence."[27] It is therefore important in determining the content of the common law we have adopted from England on the enforcement of charitable trusts to distinguish between (a) the adoptable judicial powers of the chancellor, the equity courts, and the attorney general, and (b) the nonadoptable (in America) "prerogative rights of the Crown" and the related powers of the chancellor and attorney general who were involved in the administration of those prerogative rights.[28] These powers were so interre-

---

[27] A. SCOTT *supra* note 20, § 399.1; G. BOGERT, THE LAW OF TRUSTS AND TRUSTEES § 434 (rev. 2d ed. 1977); C. ZOLLMAN, *supra* note 26, Preface and § 11.

[28] Property given for religious purposes could be given to an individual in trust for a charitable corporation or for a religious charitable use, or to a religious charitable corporation as an absolute gift for the purposes of the corporation. A third logical possibility—a gift to a religious charitable corporation in trust for a religious charitable use or another religious corporation—was originally excluded by rules of law that forbade a corporation from holding property in trust. 1 W. BLACKSTONE, COMMENTARIES *477; 2 KENT'S COMMENTARIES, *supra* note 21, at *279; Vidal v. Mayor of Philadelphia, 43 U.S. (2 How.) 127, 187 (1844) (so held "in early times . . . [but] doctrine has been long since exploded as unsound, and too artificial"). Those rules of law underline the point—overlooked in some modern cases characterizing the English common law—that if property was held by a religious corporation at common law, it was not held in trust.

lated that it is extremely difficult to untangle them for purposes of valid separate generalizations.

The powers exercised by the Crown with respect to charities, powers which were generally delegated to the chancellor to be exercised at the initiative of the attorney general, were predominantly prerogative powers. That is, the enforcement powers exercised under this heading grew not out of judicial powers but out of the royal prerogatives as *parens patriae* for the public interests, patron of charities, and head of the established church.[29] With respect to charities, these prerogative powers were exercised in at least three circumstances: (1) when property was given for a purpose which would have been charitable except for the fact that it was illegal (such as a gift for a religion other than the established church), (2) when property was given "to charity" without naming trustees or identifying a specific charitable purpose, and (3) in other cases in which the Crown acted as *parens patriae* in the public interest.

In the first two circumstances the Crown could exercise its royal prerogative as *parens patriae* by designating "in writing over his signature or sign manual the disposition which he wished to make of the property, and the chancellor would thereupon order that disposition to be made."[30] In his great work, *Equity Jurisprudence*, Joseph Story gives the same two examples and, speaking of the second example, states that a gift "to charity" will be considered "as a personal trust devolved upon the King" to be administered either by the chancellor, "as the special delegate of the Crown," or by the King acting "under

---

[29] *See generally*, TUDOR ON CHARITIES 174-76 (5th ed. Carter & Crenshaw 1929); E. FISCH, D. FREED & E. SCHACHTER, *supra* note 19, §§ 16-20. Scott says that the prerogative power was so closely associated with the judicial power (of cy pres) that it was "not entirely clear exactly where the line was to be drawn between the two situations." 4 A. SCOTT, *supra* note 20 § 399.1.

[30] 4 A SCOTT, *supra* note 20, § 399.1. A leading case discussing these two examples or prerogative powers is Jackson v. Phillips, 96 Mass. (14 Allen) 539, 574-77 (1867). *See also* C. ZOLLMAN, *supra* note 26, §§ 120-122. The sign manual was the official signature of the sovereign, affixed in a personal capacity rather than as an act of state.

the sign manual through his chancellor guiding his discretion."[31] The attorney general's role in such cases was to represent the Crown as *parens patriae* by filing an information ex officio "upon which the Lord Chancellor acts generally in the same manner and by the same proceedings as he would upon a bill in chancery."[32] Neither of these two circumstances provides any basis for enforcement powers that could be adopted into the common law of the United States.[33]

The third manifestation of royal prerogative power, which involved the crown, the chancellor, and the attorney general, concerned those diverse situations in which the King and his officers acted as *parens patriae* for the protection of those who needed special care or for the general superintending of public interests. In their search for authority to establish the attorney general's common-law power to enforce charities, American courts have often quoted the following passage from Blackstone:

> The King, as *parens patriae*, has the general superintendence of all *charities*; which he exercises by the keeper of his conscience, the chancellor. And therefore, whenever it is necessary, the attorney-general, . . . files *ex officio* an information in the court of chancery to have the charity properly established.[34]

The attorney general's clearest responsibility for "enforcement" of a

---

[31] 3 J. STORY, COMMENTARIES ON EQUITY JURISPRUDENCE § 1583, at 222 (14th ed. 1918).

[32] *Id.* at 222 n.2; 2 T. LEWIN, A PRACTICAL TREATISE ON THE LAW OF TRUSTS *927, 931 (1st Am. ed. from 8th Eng. ed. 1888). The "information in civil cases" was an ancient form of practice whereby the attorney general files a suit in equity in behalf of the government or interests under public protection, like public charities. 7A C.J.S. *Attorney General* § 11, at 835-37 (1980).

[33] The actions taken under these royal prerogative powers were sometimes quite odious, such as in the celebrated 1754 case of a devise to establish an assembly for reading the Jewish law, which was applied by royal prerogative to the support of a Christian chapel at a foundling hospital. DaCosta v. DePas, 27 Eng. Rep. 150 (Ch.1754).

[34] 3 W. BLACKSTONE, COMMENTARIES *427 *Accord*, R. BRIDGMAN, *supra* note 23, at 108 n.

charity was, therefore, at the threshold, when he filed an information in the court of chancery to obtain a decree establishing its validity.

There is a controversy over whether the attorney general's filing of an information to establish a charity was done before or only after the Statute of Charitable Uses.[35] In any event, Blackstone's above-quoted description leaves no doubt that he saw "the general superintendence of all charities," including this enforcement duty of the attorney general, as a *parens patriae* power of the Crown. And the *parens patriae* powers are generally equated with the prerogative rather than the judicial powers.[36] William Blackstone, Joseph Story, and John Marshall all grouped the Crown's *parens patriae* superintendence of charities with the prerogative rather than the judicial powers. Thus, Blackstone declares in another passage that the chancellor "is the general guardian of all infants, idiots, and lunatics; and has the general superintendence of all charitable uses in the kingdom. And all this, over and above the vast and extensive jurisdiction which he exercises in his judicial capacity in the court of chancery.... "[37] Chief Justice Marshall termed it "certain that the Crown's power to superintend and enforce charities was a branch of the royal prerogative.[38]

---

[35] Authorities for each position are discussed in E. FISCH, D. FREED & E. SCHACHTER, *supra* note 19, § 714; J. STORY, *supra* note 31, §§ 1523-1535.

[36] The inference is admittedly short of conclusive, for, as Joseph Story observed, "it is not always easy to ascertain" those cases in which the chancellor "acts as a judge administering the common duties of a Court of Equity" and those cases in which "he acts as a mere delegate of the Crown administering its peculiar duties and prerogatives." J. STORY, *supra* note 31, § 1582, at 221.

[37] 3 W. BLACKSTONE, COMMENTARIES *47. *See also id.* at *426-29, which groups superintendence of charities with the chancellor's responsibilities for infants, bankrupts and idiots, and lunatics, with the latter category being specifically described as being exercised by a warrant "issued by the king, under his royal sign manual, to the chancellor or keeper of his seal to perform his office for him." *Id.* at *427.

[38] Trustees of the Philadelphia Baptist Ass'n v. Hart's Ex'rs, 17 U.S. (4 Wheat.) 1, 47 (1819).

Story's *Equity Jurisprudence*[39] and other early treatises are to the same effect.[40]

Rendered odious in religious trusts by the intolerant positions of the Crown (as head of the established church) toward dissenting religions, the royal prerogative powers were not adopted in America.[41] Those prerogative powers had been inextricably involved in the "enforcement" and "general superintendence" of charities at the time of the Statute of Charitable Uses in 1601, and the ensuing mixture of prerogative, statutory, and judicial powers was still part of the English law when Blackstone wrote in 1765. As a result, modern American cases that rely on the common law received from England as authority for attorney general and equity court jurisdiction to "enforce" and "superintend" charities are probably in error.

The most comprehensive discussion of the English law of trusts at about the time of the creation of this nation, as seen from this side of the Atlantic, is Story's *Equity Jurisprudence*. From his perspective of time and place, Story saw two sources of authority for the enforcement and supervisory actions of the chancellor at the instance of the

---

39

> [T]here are many cases (as we shall also see) in which the jurisdiction exercised over charities in England can scarcely be said to belong to the Court of Chancery as a Court of Equity, and where it is to be treated as a personal delegation of authority to the chancellor or as an act of the Crown through the instrumentality of that dignitary.

J. STORY, *supra* note 31, § 1580, at 220. *See also id.* §§ 1581-1589, at 221-27, and §§ 1742-1752, at 361-70.

[40] The Supreme Court quoted Cooper, an early treatise writer, as saying, " 'the jurisdiction, however, in the three cases of infants, idiots or lunatics, and charitites, does not belong to the Court of Chancery as a court of equity, but as administering the prerogative and duties of the crown.' " Trustees of the Philadelphia Baptist Ass'n v. Hart's Ex'rs, 17 U.S. (4 Wheat.) 1, 48 (1819); H. BALLOW, A TREATISE OF EQUITY, pt. 2, at 209 (Fonblanque ed. 1793); 1 E. DANIEL, PLEADING AND PRACTICE OF THE HIGH COURT OF CHANCERY 7-8 (4th Am. ed. 1871).

[41] *See* authorities cited at note 27 *supra*; 2 J. PERRY, A TREATISE ON THE LAW OF TRUSTS AND TRUSTEES §§ 708, 713, 718 (6th ed. Howe 1911); Jackson v. Phillips, 96 Mass. (14 Allen) 539, 575 (1867); Gallego's Ex'rs. v. Attorney General, 30 Va. (3 Leigh) 690, 701 (1832).

attorney general, one prerogative and one judicial or common law. As to the latter, he said it was "clear upon principle" that the court of chancery "merely in virtue of its general jurisdiction over trusts" had a "right to enforce the due performance of charitable bequests" which was independent of its statutory authority and prerogative powers. This jurisdiction of the equity courts was "derived from their general authority to carry into execution the trusts of a will or other instrument according to the intention expressed in that will or instrument."[42] This presupposed a valid charitable trust, one that Story describes as "definite in its objects and lawful in its creation," which is to be "executed and regulated by trustees whether they are private individuals or a corporation." In that circumstance, Story declares, "the administration properly belongs to such trustees, and the King as *parens patriae* has no general authority to regulate or control the administration of the funds."[43] Here the *parens patriae* power is of course cited in contrast to the regular process of charitable trust administration. This further emphasizes the fact that the Crown's power to "regulate or control the administration of the funds" was not a common-law power exercisable by the attorney general.

The common-law enforcement or superintending powers were defined by Story as follows:

> In all such cases [of charitable trusts] however, if there be any abuse or misuse of the funds by the trustees, the Court of Chancery will interpose, at the instance of the attorney-general or the parties in interest, to correct such abuse or misuse of the funds. But in such cases the interposition of the court is properly referable to its general jurisdiction, as a Court of Equity, to prevent abuses of a trust, and not to any original right to direct the management of a charity or the conduct of the trustees.[44]

The distinction between the permissible interposition "to correct abuse or misuse of the funds" by the trustee and the impermissible direction of "the management of a charity or the conduct of the trustees" is the critical distinction that limits the common-law powers of

---

[42] J. STORY, *supra* note, § 1580, at 220.

[43] *Id.* § 1584, at 1223.

[44] *Id.* § 1584, at 223-24.

the attorney general and the powers of the court of chancery through which he proceeds. The reference to "abuse or misuse" seems to recognize equity and attorney general power to prevent funds devoted to a religious use from being diverted from their charitable purpose, such as by trustee embezzlements of application to a nonreligious use. But the reference to charity "management" or trustee "conduct" seems to exclude the supervision of trustee decisions within the broad limits of an honest discretion in pursuit of the specified religious use.

Thus, the American cases that rely on the English common law as the precedent for allowing the attorney general to enforce and supervise charities are erroneous. Acting under its general sovereignty, including its succession to the *parens patriae* authority of the English Crown, a state legislature may of course enact statutes conferring such broad enforcement and supervisory authority on the equity court and the attorney general, but such authority does not come from the common law.

2. The statutory enforcement authority of commissioners

The Statute of Charitable Uses gave the chancellor authority to appoint commissioners to inquire into breaches of trust, frauds, or other misapplications or abuses of charitable bequests or donations, and to make corrective decrees reviewable by the chancellor.[45] This jurisdiction was in addition to the authority under which the attorney general filed an original proceeding in the court of chancery pursuant to the preexisting prerogative or judicial powers exercised by that office.[46] The very fact that Parliament thought it necessary to create a new jurisdiction and to authorize a new enforcing authority by this legislation shows that judicial and attorney general powers of enforcement and supervision were of doubtful existence or efficacy even in 1601. In any case, the procedure of appointing commissioners was extensively employed for a time, but gradually fell into disuse

---

[45] 1601, 43 Eliz. 1, c. 4 (1601). The procedure under this law is discussed in R. BRIDGMAN, *supra* note 23, at 1-107.

[46] Attorney-General v. Mayor of Dublin, 4 Eng. Rep. 888, 902 (H.L. 1827); Note, *supra* note 26, 439-40.

and became obsolete before 1800.[47] By the time the colonies broke off from England, the attorney general had come to exercise the key role in the "enforcement" of charitable trusts, through proceedings in chancery.[48] As already noted,[49] the attorney general's role in this respect was authorized by the Crown's *parens patriae* powers, which were not adopted in America.

3. The enforcement authority of visitors

The fifth group of officials involved in the enforcement of charitable dispositions was only concerned with charitable corporations. These officials and their corporations were almost entirely free from the authority and supervision of the chancellor and attorney general. The charter or act of Parliament creating a charitable corporation generally made provisions for its governance. This was usually by the designation of "visitors" (sometimes called "governors"), who were the donor and his heirs or assigns, or the Crown if so designated or if the donor or his heirs could not be found. The visitorial power of the Crown was exercised by the Lord Chancellor. These parties, in the exercise of their "visitorial powers," supervised the government of the charity.[50]

In the leading case of *Attorney-General v. Middleton*,[51] decided in 1751, the court of chancery defined its limited enforcement powers with respect to a charitable corporation. *Middleton* involved an information brought by the attorney general against the master and governors of a school, incorporated by charter of the Crown. Relying on

---

[47] Ludlow (Corp. of) v. Greenhouse, 4 Eng. Rep. 780, 795-96 (H.L. 1827); 4 A. SCOTT,*supra* note 20, § 348.2; 2 T. LEWIN,*supra* note 32, at *927; J. STORY,*supra* note 31 § 1548.

[48] *See* authorities cited at note 47 *supra*. TUDOR ON CHARITIES,*supra* note 29, at 342-43.

[49] *See* text accompanying notes 27-44 *supra*.

[50] 1 T. LEWIN,*supra* note 32, at *528, 530, 599; TUDOR ON CHARITIES, *supra* note 29, at 194-210; 1 W. BLACKSTONE,COMMENTARIES *480-84. The person who gave "the first gift of the revenues" was the founder; later gifts did not merit that status. 1 W. BLACKSTONE,COMMENTARIES *481.

[51] 28 Eng. Rep. 210 (Ch. 1751).

what he called his "general superintendency of all charitable donations and trusts,"[52] the attorney general sought to remove the master
and compel the "trustees" to account. In ordering the information
dismissed, because chancery lacked jurisdiction for "rectifying and
regulating what is wrong in the exercise of the power of this charity,"[53] the Lord Chancellor contrasted this circumstance with that of
a "charitable use" (trust), as to which "this court exercised jurisdiction
of charities at large. . . . [B]ut where there is a charter with proper
powers, there is no ground to come into this court to establish that
charity; and it must be left to be regulated in the manner that the
charter has put it, or by the original rule of law."[54] The Lord Chancellor concluded from the evidence "that this information, though
with a plausible appearance on the face, is upon as slight grounds and
as wrong motives, as ever were known."[55]

Though decided after the founding of the United States, the subsequent chancery decision in *Attorney General v. The Governors of the
Foundling Hospital*[56] is also valuable in emphasizing the special independent status of a charity established as a charitable corporation.
In *Foundling Hospital*, the attorney general sought to enjoin the gov-

---

[52] *Id.* at 211.

[53] *Id.*

[54] *Id. Accord*, Attorney General v. Talbot, 26 Eng. Rep. 1181, 1186-87
(Ch. 1747). In declining relief in this challenge to an election to a vacant fellowship in the college, the Lord Chancellor declared:

> [I]f . . . colleges are liable to informations in this court, on the foot
> of general charities, and accountable for misapplications and
> abuses, I am afraid it would open a door to great vexation and ex-
> pense. . . . [T]he general powers of a visitor are well known; no court
> of law or equity can anticipate their judgment or take away their ju-
> risdiction, but their determinations are final and conclusive.

Id.

[55] 28 Eng. Rep. at 211.

[56] There are three different reports of this case. Listed in descending order of completeness they are 30 Eng. Rep. 514 (Ch. 1793); 29 Eng. Rep. 833
(Ch. 1793); 34 Eng. Rep. 760 (Ch. 1793).

ernors of a charitable corporation established by letters patent confirmed by act of Parliament from building on or leasing lands it owned adjacent to its hospital. The attorney general alleged that the proposed construction would have an adverse effect on the health of the children, that it involved unnecessary risk to the charity, that the resulting revenues were not necessary for the charity's operations, and that the terms of the contract were improvident. He argued that "wherever trustees of a charity were doing what was detrimental to the charity, or inconsistent with its proper objects" or "wherever trustees of a charity abused the trusts, the Court would enjoin.... "[57] The court of chancery ruled against the attorney general without even hearing his opposition. Lord Commissioner Eyre's opinion is the most explicit:

> There is nothing better established, than that this Court does not entertain a general jurisdiction to regulate and controul [sic] charities established by charter. There the establishment is fixed and determined; and the Court has no power to vary it. If the Governors, established for the regulation of it, are not those, who have the management of the revenues, this Court has no jurisdiction; and, if it is ever so much abused, as far as respects the jurisdiction of this Court, it is without remedy.... [58]

The opinion remarks that the court will, however, exercise jurisdiction "to compel a due application" where there is "a trust ... as to the application of the revenue."[59] In view of earlier rulings, these references to chancery jurisdiction over the "management of the revenues" apparently concern circumstances in which the corporation has been given property on an express trust to further some one of

---

[57] 29 Eng. Rep. at 834.

[58] 30 Eng. Rep. at 516. A different report of this same ruling reads, "Questions, therefore, which properly fall under the cognizance of the visitor of a charitable foundation, cannot be decided by a Court of Equity, nor the decision of the visitor, however erroneous, be altered, upon a bill or information." 34 Eng. Rep. at 761. *Accord*, Attorney-General v. Dulwich College, 49 Eng. Rep. 337 (M.R. 1841); TUDOR ON CHARITIES, *supra* note 29, at 178-79, 196, 206-07.

[59] 34 Eng. Rep. at 761; 30 Eng. Rep. at 516.

its corporate purposes[60] and situations in which equity would intervene to compel the restoration to the corporation of property misapplied by one of its officials.[61]

English religious corporations were also governed by visitors, but because of the established church the visitor for a corporation related to a particular level of the church was not the donor or his heirs but the next higher official in the ecclesiastical hierarchy that descended from the Crown or the chancellor through the archbishop to the bishops and the local pastors and vicars.[62] This ecclesiastical visitorial mechanism provides no precedent for the government of charitable corporations—even religious charitable corporation—in the United States. The most relevant source of common-law precedents on judicial supervision of charitable eleemosynary corporations in the United States are therefore the English cases involving schools and hospitals, discussed above.

It appears from the cases discussed in this section that at the time of the founding of the United States, the English court of chancery and attorney general had no general common-law supervisory or regulatory powers over charitable *corporations*,[63] and that their jurisdiction to intervene in the application of corporate revenues was limited to correcting embezzlements. Moreover, their supervisory

---

[60] Attorney-General v. Governors of Harrow School, 28 Eng. Rep. 351 (Ch. 1754) (information entertained because it concerned "a distinct charity from the school, a collateral trust" to repair needed roads, of which the governors were trustees and could therefore be compelled, just like other charitable trustees, to apply the revenue for the designated purpose rather than to the entire range of its charitable activities).

[61] Attorney-General v. Corporation of Bedford, 28 Eng. Rep. 323 (Ch. 1754) (chancery's power to act on "the management of the revenue of this school" used to order master to account to corporation for funds misappropriated to personal purposes).

[62] 1 W. BLACKSTONE, COMMENTARIES *480-84.

[63] After 1800, the English law's reliance upon the supervisory functions of visitors and governors declined, and judicial decisions and writers began to concede chancery and the attorney general a limited supervisory function over the management as well as the revenues of a charitable corporation. *E.g.*, Attorney-General v. St. Cross Hosp., 51 Eng. Rep. 1103 (M.R. 1853); Attorney-General v. Earl of Clarendon, 34 Eng. Rep. 190 (Ch. 1810);

power over charitable *trusts* was not a judicial power, but was almost entirely associated with the prerogative powers of the Crown, which were not suitable for adoption into the altered circumstances existing in a new nation founded on religious freedom and nonestablishment.

B. CHURCH PROPERTY DISPUTES

The English courts' employment of trust theories as a basis for resolving disputes between contending factions to church property is necessarily more recent. Before Henry VIII established the Church of England in 1534 and, indeed, before the Restoration in 1660, disputes between contending religious factions were settled in ecclesiastical courts or on the battlefield. Noncomformist groups were allowed to exist after 1660, and it was their newly accumulated property and inevitable doctrinal controversies that gave the English courts their first experience with trust doctrines in church property disputes. Since the first cases were not decided until after the American Revolution, it is accurate to say that there was no received English common law on this subject, but the English decisions of the early 1800s were influential on this side of the Atlantic and are therefore worthy of review.

The first court test arose, inevitably, among the dissenters in Scotland. In 1731 a group who considered themselves the only genuine Presbyterians broke with the Church of Scotland and established a similar church judicatory under the name "Associate Synod of Burgher Seceders." A congregation subject to this Synod contributed funds to buy land and build a chapel. In 1795 the congregation split over a doctrinal dispute. In a contest over ownership of the chapel, the Associate Synod, the church's judicatory, ruled for the congregational majority, who had adopted what the House of Lords later termed "the new or innovating doctrines," as against the claims of the minority (allegedly a majority of the original contributors) who were "adhering to the original faith of their sect. . . . " The Scottish

---

1 T. LEWIN, *supra* note 32, at *528-30 (court can intervene when administration of corporate property by the governors would "pervert the end of the institution").

Court of Session, almost equally divided, sustained the ecclesiastical decision, but in *Craigdallie v. Aikman*[64] the House of Lords sent the case back for further review and decision, informed by the Lord Chancellor's observations on five issues of importance in the case: (1) an express trust for the original contributors and their heirs would be extremely difficult if not impossible to apply;[65] (2) "[i]f it were distinctly intended that the Synod should direct the use of the property, that ought to have been matter of contract,"[66] which apparently had not been done here; (3) the court might "take notice of religious opinions," not "with a view to decide whether they were right or wrong," but "as facts pointing out the ownership of property;"[67] (4) here the property had been contributed to and could be understood as being held in trust for "a society then agreeing in their religious opinions adhered to a Presbytery or Synod then holding the same opinions with themselves,"[68] (5) the law of England would not "execute the trust for a religious society, at the expense of a forfeiture of their property by the *cestui que* trusts, for adhering to the opinions and principles in which the congregation had originally united."[69]

Unable to find any intelligible difference of opinion between the contending factions on remand, the Court of Session denied relief to the minority who had separated themselves from the Associate Synod. In an opinion expressing the House of Lords affirmance of that action, the Lord Chancellor gave this explanation of the ruling principles in this much-cited case:

> When this matter was formerly before the House, we acted upon this principle, that if we could find out what were the religious principles of those who originally attended the chapel, we should hold the building appropriated to the use of persons who adhere to the same

---

[64] 3 Eng. Rep. 601, 602 (H.L. 1813).

[65] *Id.* at 606.

[66] *Id.*

[67] *Id.*

[68] *Id.*

[69] *Id.*

religious principles. . . . And supposing that there is a division of religious opinions in the persons at present wishing to enjoy this building, the question then would be, which of them adhered to the opinions of those who had built the place of worship, and which of them differed from those opinions? Those who still adhered to those religious principles being more properly to be considered as the *cestui que* trusts of those who held this place of worship in trust, than those who have departed altogether from the religious principles of those who founded this place, if I may so express it.[70]

The principle enunciated in *Craigdallie v. Aikman* came to be known as the "implied trust" doctrine. Even though there was no evidence of an express trust provision or intent on the part of those who originally provided that property and funds for the church building, the court would apply a legal fiction to the effect that the title was held on an "implied trust" for the benefit of those who adhered to the religious principles of opinions of the donors, as against those persons who had departed therefrom. This doctrine was applied in several other cases, the first of which was decided by the same Lord Chancellor sitting in chancery.

In *Attorney-General v. Pearson*[71] a meeting house erected by Presbyterians in 1701 under a trust deed referring to its purpose as "the worship and service of God"[72] came into controversy eighty years later when a portion of the congregation and its new minister adopted Unitarianism and abandoned teaching the doctrine of the Holy Trinity. The attorney general, on the relation of those who contended that the original purpose was for promoting "the doctrine of the Holy Trinity," brought a bill to quiet title and appoint new trustees. Lord Eldon declared it settled that if property were given "in such a way that the purpose be clearly expressed to be that of maintaining a society of Protestant Dissenters . . . it is then the duty of this Court to carry such a trust as that into execution, and to administer it

---

[70] Craigdallie v. Aikman, 4 Eng. Rep. 435, 439-40 (H.L. 1820).

[71] 36 Eng. Rep. 135 (Ch. 1817).

[72] *Id*. at 136.

according to the intent of the founders."[73] In this case there was nothing in the deeds to inform the court "what species of [Protestant dissenting] doctrine this institution was intended to maintain."[74] Consequently, the chancellor granted a staying injunction and referred the case to a master to inquire into the nature of the doctrines and worship for which the charitable estate had been created.[75] This inquiry had not been concluded when the case came back to chancery in 1835. This time the court concluded that the Presbyterians who founded the charity "never could have meant that that particular doctrine [of Unitarianism, which denied the Trinity] should be taught in this chapel as part of the worship and service of God."[76] As a result, the vice chancellor declared, the decree "ought to be so framed as to exclude those particular doctrines which the information complains of from being preached in the chapel," and to prohibit persons who maintained such opinions from serving as trustees of the chapel.[77]

This precedent was followed in another case, which turned on the meaning of the words "poor and godly preachers of Christ's Holy Gospel" in a charity founded by Lady Hewley. Characterizing her as a Presbyterian, "a Trinitarian, and a believer in the doctrine of Original Sin,"[78] the chancellor concluded that "she never intended that her bounty should be applied for the purpose of promoting or en-

---

[73] *Id.* at 153. The special position of the established church is evident in Lord Eldon's statement that if property were given in trust with no more precise instruction than for "propagating the worship of God . . . this Court would execute such a trust, by making it a provision for maintaining and propagating the Established Religion of the country." *Id.*

[74] *Id.* at 154.

[75] *Id.* at 157.

[76] Attorney-General v. Pearson, 58 Eng. Rep. 848, 855 (V.C. 1835).

[77] *Id.* at 855.

[78] Attorney-General v. Shore, 58 Eng. Rep. 855, 857 (Ch. 1836). This opinion is also quoted in its entirety in the report of the appeal before the House of Lords. Shore v. Wilson, 8 Eng. Rep. 450, 466-72 (H.L. 1842).

couraging the preaching of Unitarian doctrines."[79] Trustees who were Unitarians and had manifested a strong "leaning" in favor of other Unitarians were removed in the court's fulfillment of what it saw as its duty "to give effect to the intent of the founder. . . ."[80]

In this manner the doctrine of implied trust in the settlement of church property disputes involved the English court of chancery and the attorney general in the content and enforcement of religious doctrine and belief to an extent that would need to be recognized as inappropriate for the courts of a nation without an established church.

---

[79] 58 Eng. Rep. at 858.

[80] *Id.* at 856. For subsequent opinions showing how the attorney general and the courts struggled with the intricacies of religious doctrine and belief in efforts to determine who could serve as trustees and who could benefit from the trust, see Shore v. Wilson, 8 Eng. Rep. 450 (H.L. 1842) (in effect affirming the chancellor's decision reported above as to the ineligibility of Unitarians); Attorney-General v. Shore, 59 Eng. Rep. 1002 (V.C. 1843).

III

THE COMMON LAW
OF RELIGIOUS TRUSTS
AND CORPORATIONS
IN THE UNITED STATES

Writing in 1765, William Blackstone observed that the colonists in the "distant plantations in America" carried with them "only so much of the English law, as [was] applicable to their own situation."[81] The adoption of English common law in the various American states was in accordance with that flexibility and was predictably diverse in detail from state to state. Some states adopted the common law as of the time of settlement, others as of the Revolution, but none adopted it entirely. Sitting on circuit in 1798, Justice Samuel Chase declared:

> When the *American* colonies were first settled by our ancestors . . . they brought hither, as a birth-right and inheritance, so much of the common law, as was applicable to their local situation, and change of

---

[81] 1 W. BLACKSTONE, COMMENTARIES *107-08. For example, "the mode of maintenance for the established clergy, the jurisdiction of spiritual courts, and a multitude of other provisions, are neither necessary nor convenient for them, and therefore are not in force." *Id*. at 108.

circumstances. But each colony judged for itself, what parts of the common law were applicable to its new condition; and in various modes, by Legislative acts, by Judicial decisions, or by constant usage, adopted some parts, and rejected others.[82]

In Pennsylvania the judges of the supreme court gave this response to a formal inquiry from the General Assembly about which English statutes were in force in the Commonwealth:

It is the true principle of colonization, that the emigrants from the mother country carry with them such laws as are useful in their new situation, and none other. A multitude of *English* statutes, relating to the king's prerogative, the rights and privileges of the nobility and clergy, the local commerce and revenue of *England*, and other subjects unnecessary to enumerate, were improper to be extended to *Pennsylvania*.[83]

Predictably, the English laws relating to royal prerogative rights and the established church were not adopted in this country. The common law that the English attorney general used in his supervision of charitable trusts and in his role in resolving church property disputes was inextricably interwoven with royal prerogatives and with judicial review of religious doctrine, both odious concepts in a nation committed to religious freedom and against a national established church.

In a nation so committed it was inevitable that there would be property controversies arising out of schisms over religious doctrines. The first section of this part will review how American courts have applied common-law trust doctrines in resolving these church

---

[82] United States v. Worrall, 2 U.S. (2 Dall.) 384, 394 (C.C.Pa. 1798), *See generally* Dale, *The Adoption of the Common Law by the American Colonies*, 21 AM. L. REG. (N.S.) 553 (1882).

[83] *Report of the Judges of the Supreme Court to the Senate and House of Representatives*, 3 Binn. 593 (Pa. 1810-1811), *quoted in* S. KIMBALL, HISTORICAL INTRODUCTION TO THE LEGAL SYSTEM 289-90 (1966). Similarly, California adopted the common law in its initial statutory codification. CALIF. CIV. CODE § 22.2 (West 1978). In 1850 a California Senate Committee on the Judiciary explained "that in cases not falling within the Constitution of the United States, or the Constitution or statutes of this State, the Courts shall be governed in their adjudications by the English Common Law, as received and modified in the United States; in other words, by the American Common Law." *Report on Civil and Common Law*, 1 Cal. 588 (1850), *quoted in* S. KIMBALL, *supra*, at 311, 314-15.

property disputes. The second section will examine the history of judicial and attorney general enforcement and supervisory authority over religious charitable trusts and corporations.

A. CHURCH PROPERTY DISPUTES

As noted in the preceding part, the dominant English legal doctrine for resolving church property disputes in the nineteenth century was the implied trust doctrine, by which money and other property contributed to a church was deemed impressed with a trust for the benefit of those who adhered to the religious doctrines and principles of the donors of the church at the time of its founding. American judicial application of this doctrine can be seen in three phases. In the first phase most courts rejected the implied trust doctrine as unsuited to the separation of church and state and to the freedom of religion guaranteed in the new nation. Gradually, however, most state courts came to apply the doctrine of implied trust, until in the second phase it was a dominant force for over a century. Then, in 1969 and 1979, the United States Supreme Court rejected the doctrine as unconstitutional[84] The state courts are now entering a third phase, groping for substitute legal doctrines for resolving church property disputes.

American church property disputes have involved three general types of church organizations; (1) congregational, involving a relatively independent self-governing congregation, like the Baptist Church; (2) hierarchical-episcopal, involving authority vested in ecclesiastical officers at successive levels, like the Roman Catholic Church; and (3) hierarchical-synodical or associational, involving authority delegated to democratically elected bodies exercising power at successive levels, like the Presbyterian Church.[85] The prop-

---

[84] Presbyterian Church v. Mary E. B. Hull Memorial Presbyterian Church, 393 U.S. 440 (1969); Jones v. Wolf, 443 U.S. 595 (1979), discussed in text accompanying notes 355-56 *infra*.

[85] *See* Kauper, *Church Autonomy and the First Amendment: The Presbyterian Church Case*, 1969 SUP. CT. REV. 347, 354; Note, *Judicial Intervention in Disputes Over the Use of Church Property*, 75 HARV. L. REV. 1142, 1143-44 (1962); Comment, *Judicial Intervention in Church Property Disputes—Some Constitutional Considerations*, 74 YALE L.J. 1113 (1965). For a discussion of court decisions classifying various denominations, see Annot., 52 A.L.R.3d 324, 381-427 (1973).

erty involved in these disputes is most often the product of member contributions not expressly donated in trust or even restricted to any particular purpose, but the cases occasionally concern an express trust or a restricted gift from a single donor or group of donors.

The implied trust doctrine was not articulated by the English courts until 1817, and did not emerge in judicial opinions in the United States until several decades thereafter. The first half of the nineteenth century was a period of aggressive independence. The American states were reveling in majority rule, freeing themselves from unpopular English institutions like the established churches that persisted in a few states, and experiencing theological revolutions like the Unitarian conquest of Congregational churches in New England.[86] The decisions growing out of property controversies between Congregational and Unitarian factions in Massachusetts provided what was apparently the first body of American common law on this subject, but these cases were not very helpful as precedents because they were entangled with the dying remnants of the official church establishment in that state.[87] In other cases decided in the 1830s, involving Lutheran and Baptist schisms in North Carolina and Ohio, the courts gave short shrift to arguments that the church property should be decreed to the minority when the majority had departed from the original doctrine. Without specific mention of the implied trust doctrine, but in a clear rejection of its underlying principle and in a strong endorsement of congregational autonomy and democracy, these courts held that church property was subject to the will of the congregational majority.[88]

---

[86] The Unitarian controversy is discussed in L. LEVY, THE LAW OF THE COMMONWEALTH AND CHIEF JUSTICE SHAW ch. 3 (1957).

[87] *E.g.*, Baker v. Fales, 16 Mass. 487 (1820); Stebbins v. Jennings, 27 Mass. (10 Pick.) 171 (1830), *discussed in* L. LEVY, *supra* note 86, at 30-35; Levy, *Chief Justice Shaw and the Church Property Controversy in Massachusetts*, 30 B.U.L. REV. 219 (1950). These cases held that the title holder of the church property was the territorial parish, a public corporation that levied on its inhabitants to support the established church. Massachusetts disestablished its church in 1833. L. LEVY, *supra* note 86, at 32-42.

[88] Trustees of the Organ Meeting House v. Seaford, 16 N.C. (1 Dev. Eq.) 453 (1830); Keyser v. Stansifer, 6 Ohio 364 (1834).

The earliest extensive discussion and evaluation of the English implied trust precedents was in *Smith v. Nelson*,[89] an 1846 opinion in the Vermont Supreme Court. This case involved a testamentary gift to the "trustee" of an unincorporated religious society "the interest thereof to be annually paid to their minister forever." A schism in the congregation raised doubts over which minister qualified, different parties contended for payment of the legacy and interest, and the controversy moved into a court of equity. In a long and diffuse opinion the court struggled for an acceptable rationale to resolve such disputes.

The strikingly different situation in England, where the Crown was the head of the established church and ecclesiastical courts and ecclesiastical law were part of the common law, had no counterpart in this country because of "our constitutional provisions in relation to religious freedom."[90] Consequently, the Court said, the kind of judicial examination of religious doctrines involved in English cases, such as *Attorney-General v. Pearson*, "could not . . . be tolerated in this country."[91] The devise was held to be a gift for the benefit of the congregation, not a gift on an implied trust for the adherents to some particular doctrine. The court ordered that that legacy be paid to the trustees elected by the congregation, with interest to the minister they had selected.[92]

The most influential rejection of the implied trust doctrine in the nineteenth century was in the 1854 New York Court of Appeals decision, *Robertson v. Bullions*.[93] In this property dispute the faction whose position had been sustained by the synod sought equitable relief to remove the trustees of the incorporated religious society and to require them to account for their management of the church property. Justice Selden's opinion outlines the two contending positions

---

[89] 18 Vt. 202, 214 (1846).

[90] *Id*. at 220.

[91] *Id. Accord*, J. STORY, *supra* note 31, at 225 n.1.

[92] 18 Vt. at 225-26.

[93] 11 N.Y. 243 (1854).

on the legal effect of the legislative act incorporating the religious society. Specifically, (1) did the act incorporate the church *trustees*, so that the corporation held the church property in charitable trust for the members and purposes of the church (a voluntary association)? or (2) did it incorporate the religious *society*, without trust relationships? The court rejected the first (trustee) position because this would "devolve upon the courts of equity the administration of the entire property of religious corporations through the state," with consequent involvement in religious doctrine.[94] This decision, an important doctrinal landmark in establishing the autonomy of religious corporations and in explaining why the attorney general has only minimal supervisory powers over them, is discussed in the next section.[95]

The second part of the court's opinion answered the argument that the religious corporation received its gifts upon a trust for its corporate purposes, which were implied in "*the tenets, faith and practice of the creators of the fund.*"[96] In sternly rejecting this attempt to implant the implied trust doctrine, as defined in the English case of *Attorney-General v. Pearson*, the court criticized the American courts by which this doctrine had been "so frequently cited and so much relied upon":

> That it so proves, that our courts have not always reflected upon the difference in this respect, between a country where all religions, at least all forms of the Christian religion, are tolerated and placed upon an equal footing, and one where a particular form of worship is established by law. The case under review, considering the nature of the point decided in it, is *wholly* without weight in this country; because we have no religious system to which it can apply.[97]

As the leading case expounding what might be called "the corporate autonomy" model, *Robertson v. Bullions* stands for the proposition that, in the absence of some specific express trust provision to the

---

[94] *Id.* at 247. The importance of this decision in the context of the American law of religious corporations is noted in Kauper & Ellis, *Religious Corporations and the Law*, 71 MICH. L. REV. 1500, 1511-12 (1973).

[95] *See* text accompanying notes 185-90 *infra*.

[96] 11 N.Y. at 256 (emphasis in the original).

[97] *Id.* at 259.

contrary, religious charitable corporations do not hold their property in trust for the support of a particular doctrine, denomination, or membership. Corporate officials, typically the trustees or deacons elected by the congregation, have complete control over the corporation's property, without the limitation of trust obligations and without regard to religious doctrines, affiliations, or practices.

The next leading case in this line of authority was the United States Supreme Court's first case involving a church property dispute. *Watson v. Jones*,[98] decided in 1871, involved the ownership of a Presbyterian Church in Louisville, Kentucky, whose members had divided over the slavery issue. The highest judicatory body in this hierarchical church ruled for the anti-slavery contestants, and the federal circuit court, applying common-law principles, gave the requested injunctive relief to secure their position. In the Supreme Court, appellant's counsel relied on *Craigdallie v. Aikman* and other English precedents[99] to argue that the trustees (incorporated under the state law) who held legal title to this church property held it in trust for the local congregation, subject to the church's system of doctrines and rules as interpreted by the civil court rather than the church judicatory. The Supreme Court disagreed:

> [I]n cases of this character we are bound to look at the fact that the local congregation is itself but a member of a much larger and more important religious organization, and is under its government and control, and is bound by its orders and judgments.
>
> . . . [W]henever the question of discipline, or of faith, or ecclesiastical rule, custom, or law have been decided by the highest of these church judicatories to which the matter has been carried, the legal tribunals must accept such decisions as final, and as binding on them, in their application to the case before them.[100]

The Supreme Court conceded that the English decisions, which made their own rulings on religious doctrine and practice, were contrary, but attributed this to the different role of the judiciary in a

---

[98] 80 U.S. (13 Wall.) 679 (1871), *discussed in* Kauper, *supra* note 85, at 357-64; Comment, *supra* note 85, at 1113-19.

[99] Discussed in text accompanying notes 64-80 *supra*.

[100] 80 U.S. at 726-27.

country with an established church, in contrast to this country, where religious freedom is guaranteed and exercised."[101]

The holding in *Watson v. Jones* rejected the English doctrine of implied trust by deferring to the decisions of church judicatory bodies. The Court could readily do this in the context of the hierarchical church involved in that case. In addition, in an obvious attempt to provide guidance to a state and federal judiciary groping to find appropriate principles to decide property controversies involving a variety of church polities, the Supreme Court offered two notable dicta that pertained to disputes in churches with other types of governance. First, when "a strictly congregational or independent organization, governed solely within itself," holds property acquired by purchase or donation "with no other specific trust attached to it in the hands of the church than that it is for the use of that congregation as a religious society," the ownership rights of contending parties "must be determined by the ordinary principles which govern voluntary associations." If no trust was imposed upon the property when purchased or given, the court will not find an implied one to take the property from those entitled under regular succession merely because they have changed their religious opinions.[102] This was an outright rejection of the implied trust doctrine in its application to congregational as well as hierarchical churches. Second, when property has been "dedicate[d] by way of trust to the purpose of sustaining, supporting and propagating definite religious doctrines or principles" and when the governing instrument contains "the formalities which the laws require," the courts will "see that the property so dedicated is not diverted from the trust which is thus attached to its use" regardless of the congregational or hierarchical government of the church or the majority or minority status of those who adhere to the original doctrines. In other words, a formally created express trust will be honored in ecclesiastical matters, just as with other charities.[103]

---

[101] *Id*. at 726-28.

[102] *Id*. at 724-25.

[103] *Id*. at 723. The express trust exception is discussed briefly in Note, *supra* note 85, at 1156-57, 1168.

Each of these dicta was consistent with prior state decisions rejecting the doctrine of implied trust and promoting church corporate autonomy and majority rule as governing principles in church property controversies.[104] But despite its great influence otherwise, *Watson v. Jones'* rejection of the implied trust doctrine proved unpersuasive to state courts, which still had the final word on the content of the common law in this area. In the decade preceding *Watson v. Jones* at least four state supreme courts had embraced the implied trust doctrine, some in more than one case.[105] The doctrine was too convenient and the momentum too strong to be reversed by a dictum of the United States Supreme Court.

In the earliest American cases applying the implied trust doctrine in the resolution of church property disputes, the courts did so in support of rulings in favor of the factions that adhered to the hierarchical church organizations with which the congregations had been affiliated. This fact emphasized the courts' reliance on the churches' own judicatory bodies and minimized the courts' inquiry into religious doctrines. In this factual circumstance the implied trust enforced a continuity of denominational affiliation as much or more than a continuity of religious tenets.[106]

The Pennsylvania Supreme Court, which had previously rejected the implied trust doctrine,[107] provided an excellent example of the trend toward use of this doctrine in its 1870 decision in *Schnorr's*

---

[104] Trustees of the Organ Meeting House v. Seaford, 16 N.C. (1 Dev. Eq.) 453 (1830); Robertson v. Bullions, 11 N.Y. 243 (1854); Keyser v. Stansifer, 6 Ohio 364 (1834); McGinnis v. Watson, 41 Pa. 9 (1861); Smith v. Nelson, 18 Vt. 202 (1846).

[105] Brunnenmeyer v. Buhre, 32 Ill. 159 (1863); Ferraria v. Vasconcelles, 23 Ill. 403 (1860); First Constitutional Presbyterian Church v. Congregational Soc'y, 23 Iowa 567 (1867); McBride v. Porter, 17 Iowa 203 (1864); Hale v. Everett, 53 N.H. 9 (1868); Schnorr's Appeal, 67 Pa. 138 (1870). An earlier case apparently using the implied trust theory is Gibson v. Armstrong, 46 Ky. (7 B. Mon.). 481 (1847).

[106] Note, *supra* note 85, at 1151-52, 1167-71.

[107] McGinnis v. Watson, 41 Pa. 9 (1861), *discussed in* Note, *supra* note 85, at 1153. *But cf.* App v. Lutheran Congregation, 6 Pa. 201 (1847).

Appeal,[108] which became a leading case. This property controversy involved a church incorporated in 1865 "to worship Almighty God according to the faith and discipline of the German Evangelical Reformed church" and subject to the control of its synod in the United States. In 1866 the property in question, on which a brick church was later constructed with donated funds, was deeded to the corporation "for the use of a congregation of the German Evangelical Reformed Church, and with the condition that no change shall be made in said congregation for any other denomination."[109] The dispute arose when one faction in the congregation declared itself independent of all synods, absolved itself from the government of the German Reformed Church, and elected a pastor not connected with that church.[110] A decree securing ownership in those who adhered to the original denomination and doctrine was affirmed on appeal.

The court could easily have explained its holding as an enforcement of the express trust specified in the original deed, read in harmony with the articles of incorporation. Some of its opinion reads in this manner. Thus, the court repeatedly states that the managers of the institution cannot break off from the original doctrine or connection "[w]hen the founders or donors have clearly expressed their intention that a particular set of doctrines shall be taught, or a particular form of worship and government be maintained."[111] But the court's opinion also contains language that amounts to an application of the doctrine of implied trust. Thus, when property "is vested in a religious society, whether incorporated or not," the court said, "it is a charitable use," and "[t]he corporation or society are trustees, and can no more divert the property from the use to which it was originally dedicated, than any other trustees can."[112]

This failure to follow *Watson v. Jones*' rejection of the implied trust doctrine, coupled with a strong reliance on denominational conti-

---

[108] 67 Pa. 138 (1870).

[109] *Id.* at 139.

[110] *Id.* at 147.

[111] *Id.* at 146.

[112] *Id. Accord*, Roshi's Appeal, 69 Pa. 462 (1871).

nuity, was typical of state court decisions in the second phase, which spanned the century following *Watson v. Jones*. Court after court succumbed to the appeal of the implied trust doctrine in rulings on religious doctrine and ecclesiastical practices in a wide variety of church organizations.[113] As courts gained experience with the implied trust doctrine and recognized the desirability of some flexibility for change, imposition of the implied trust was limited to those situations in which the changes were "substantial" departures from "fundamental" doctrines.[114] This plunged the courts even deeper into religious doctrines, since the application of this modification required the courts not only to define doctrine but also to evaluate its significance in the overall theology and practice. Despite these problems, in the century preceding 1969 most courts came to apply some version of the implied trust doctrine in church property disputes, especially in congregational churches.[115]

The force of the holding in *Watson v. Jones*, deferring to the decisions of church judicatories, made hierarchical churches less susceptible to judicial interference than congregational ones, but the hierarchical churches were not free from difficulty. Under the so-

---

[113] *E.g.*, Baker v. Ducker, 79 Cal. 365 (1889), discussed in text at note 232 *infra*; Apostolic Holiness Union v. Knudson, 21 Idaho 589, 123 P. 473 (1912); Christian Church v. Church of Christ, 219 Ill. 503, 76 N.E. 703 (1906); Lindstrom v. Tell, 131 Minn. 203, 154 N.W. 969 (1915); Mount Helm Baptist Church v. Jones, 79 Miss 488 (1901); Peace v. First Christian Church, 20 Tex. Civ. App. 85, 48 S.W. 534 (1898); Marien v. Evangelical Creed Congregation, 132 Wis. 650, 113 N.W. 66 (1907); cases cited in Annot., 52 A.L.R.3d 324 (1973); Annot., 15 A.L.R.3d 297 (1967); Annot., 70 A.L.R. 75 (1931); Annot., 8 A.L.R. 105 (1920); G. BOGERT, *supra* note 27, § 398; Note, *supra* note 85, at 158-80.

[114] *E.g.*, Mack v. Kime, 129 Ga. 1, 58 S.E. 184 (1907) (clearest statement of "fundamental" change requirement); Stallings v. Finney, 287 Ill. 145, 122 N.E. 369 (1919); Christian Church v. Church of Christ, 219 Ill. 503, 76 N.E. 703 (1906); Mt. Zion Baptist Church v. Whitmore, 83 Iowa 138, 49 N.W. 81 (1891); Karoly v. Hungarian Reformed Chuch, 83 N.J. Eq. 514, 91 A. 808 (1914); Kauper, *supra* note 85, at 363; Note, *supra* note 85, at 1152, 1170-73; G. BOGERT, *supra* note 27, § 398, at 315-21.

[115] Kauper, *supra* note 85, at 351, 362-63; Note, *supra*, note 85, at 1157-58; G. BOGERT, *supra* note 27 § 398, at 315-21.

called "polity" approach, courts determined whether the relationship between the local congregation and the governing body was
congregational or one of the forms of hierarchical, and generally
awarded the property to the local congregation or the parent church
on the basis of that decision.[116] The problem with that approach was
the obscurity of the distinction between congregational and hierarchical, evident in many cases, and the fact that the necessary judicial
inquiry into the interstices of ecclesiastical government and relationships was hardly less offensive to religious freedom and nonestablishment than inquiries into doctrine, if, indeed, the two could be
distinguished.[117] This confusing state of the law, in which litigation
has flourished, has now been superseded by the Supreme Court constitutional decisions, discussed in Part VI, which federalize the
ground rules for judicial intervention in church property disputes.
Whether the Supreme Court can provide a better common law in this
area than the highest courts of several states remains to be seen.

B. JUDICIAL AND ATTORNEY GENERAL
SUPERVISORY AUTHORITY OVER
RELIGIOUS CHARITABLE TRUSTS
AND CORPORATIONS

Unlike the charitable corporation, which was apparently
adopted into American statutory and case law without serious question, the charitable trust had a troubled history because of the states'
uneven reception of English statutory and common law. After a brief
reference to that history, this section will review the American common law on supervisory authority over charitable trusts and corpo-

---

[116] *E.g.*, Bouldin v. Alexander, 82 U.S. (15 Wall.) 131 (1872); Holiman
v. Dovers, 236 Ark. 211, 366 S.W.2d 197 (1963); Smith v. Pedigo, 145 Ind.
361, 33 N.E. 777 (1893); Brunnenmeyer v. Buhre, 32 Ill. 159 (1863); First
Constitutional Presbyterian Church v. The Congregational Soc'y, 23 Iowa
567 (1867); McBride v. Porter, 17 Iowa 203 (1864); American Primitive
Soc'y, v. Pilling, 24 N.J.L. 653 (1855); App v. Lutheran Congregation, 6 Pa.
201 (1847); G. BOGERT, *supra* note 27 § 398, at 301-04; Kauper, *supra* note
85, 355-56; Note, *supra* note 85, at 1158-60; Annot., 52 A.L.R.3d 324 (1973)

[117] Kauper, *supra* note 85, at 371.

rations. The next part will describe the twentieth-century legislation on this subject.

1. The validity of charitable trusts

In the formative years of the new nation, some American states repealed a long list of English statutes, including the Statute of Charitable Uses.[118] In *Trustees of the Philadelphia Baptist Association v. Hart's Executors*,[119] Chief Justice Marshall, writing for a unanimous United States Supreme Court, held that a charitable disposition in a Virginia will could not be valid, because the attempted indefinite bequest rested entirely on a statutory foundation, the Statute of Charitable Uses, which Virginia had repealed along with other English legislation. As a result of that decision, charitable trusts were wholly or partly invalid for much of the nineteenth century in four jurisdictions having closely related systems of statutory law: the District of Columbia, Maryland, Virginia, and West Virginia.[120] In *Vidal v. Mayor of Philadelphia*[121] in 1844, Justice Joseph Story used newly discovered historical evidence to displace Marshall's conclusion by showing that "charitable uses might be enforced in chancery upon the general jurisdiction of the court, independently of the statute of 43 of Elizabeth...."[122] This ruling, which endorsed the common-law

---

[118] C. ZOLLMAN, *supra* note 26 §§ 32-107; ZOLLMAN, *The Development of the Law of Charities in the United States*, 19 COLUM. L. REV. 91 *passim* (1919); Note, *The Enforcement of Charitable Trusts in America: A History of Evolving Social Attitudes*, 54 VA. L. REV. 436,441 (1968). *See generally* H. MILLER, THE LEGAL FOUNDATIONS OF AMERICAN PHILANTHROPY 1776-1844, at 10-15 (1961).

[119] 17 U.S. (4 Wheat.) 1 (1819). *Accord*, Gallego's Ex'rs v. Attorney General, 30 Va. (3 Leigh) 690 (1832) (Virginia's statutory repeal of the validity of charitable trusts and the limit it placed on the power of church corporations attributed to the "decided hostility of the legislative power to religious incorporations" because of concerns about the accumulation of property and the exercise of political power by the clergy. *Id.* at 700-01).

[120] C. ZOLLMAN, *supra* note 26 §§ 73-107; Zollman, *supra* note 118, at 91-98; Note, *supra* note 118, at 451-55.

[121] 43 U.S. (2 How.) 127 (1844).

[122] *Id.* at 194.

origins of the charitable trust, gave substantial impetus to the validity and use of the charitable trust in many states in the United States but did not restore the charitable trust in Virginia and other states where it had been held invalid and where its restoration had to await legislative action.[123] The general repeal of English legislation in New York in 1788, followed by a new codification in 1828 that abolished uses and trusts except as provided therein and that was silent on charitable trusts, left the validity of charitable trusts subject to varying judicial construction in that state for four decades. The confusion culminated, after 1860, in the temporary invalidity (for periods of two to five decades) of charitable trusts in New York and three other states whose statutes were based on New York's: Michigan, Minnesota, and Wisconsin.[124] In most other states, by reliance on a combination of English and American statutory and common law, the validity of the charitable trust was recognized expressly or impliedly from the beginning.[125]

2. The enforcement of charitable trusts

Judicial or legislative recognition of the equity court's jurisdiction to enforce or supervise charitable trusts has come slowly in some states because its English counterpart exercised not only judicial powers but also the royal prerogative powers that were unwelcome in the new nation. The attorney general's close association with the prerogative or *parens patriae* powers of the Crown has made it even more difficult for that officer to be acknowledged as having any common-law powers in the enforcement of supervision of charitable trusts.

In *Trustees of the Philadelphia Baptist Association v. Hart's Executors*,[126] Chief Justice Marshall conceded that "the power of the crown

---

[123] 2 J. PERRY, *supra* note 41, § 694. *See also* authorities cited at note 120 *supra*.

[124] C. ZOLLMAN, *supra* note 26, §§ 47-68; Zollman, *supra* note 118, at 98-111; Note, *supra* note 118, at 455-58.

[125] C. ZOLLMAN, *supra* note 26 §§ 73-107; Zollman, *supra* note 118, at 288-309; Note, *supra* note 118, at 451; G. BOGERT, *supra* note 27, § 322.

[126] 17 U.S. (4 Wheat.) 1 (1819).

to superintend and enforce charities existed in very early times," but declared it "certain" that this "superintending power of the crown" was a "branch of the [royal] prerogative, and not a part of the ordinary [judicial] power of the chancellor. . . . "[127] Virginia's highest court agreed with this reasoning in *Gallego's Executors v. Attorney General*,[128] which held that "the jurisdiction of the chancellor of England over charities, is a branch of the prerogative, and not part of the ordinary powers of the chancery court, in the exercise of its equitable jurisdiction."[129] The court observed that "this branch of the royal prerogative, if it had not been withered by the repeal of the statute, would have devolved upon the legislature. That body [not the judiciary] is the parens patriae, under our system. . . . "[130] To the Virginia judges, and probably to others in the new nation, the chancellor's function in connection with the Crown's *parens patriae* power looked like the exercise of prerogative, not judicial power, and the whole subject of official jurisdiction over religious charitable corporations smacked of the established church and interferences with religious liberty. Both were unsuited to a nation committed by constitutional law to religious freedom and nonestablishment.

Justice Story's opinion in *Vidal v. Mayor of Philadelphia*[131] reversed Marshall's reasoning by affirming that the chancellor had an inherent common-law jurisdiction over charitable trusts. In contrast, Story clearly indicated that the attorney general's role was an extension of the royal prerogative. He quoted approvingly from an opinion of Lord Redesdale, whom he called " a great judge in equity," which stated that "the right which the attorney general has to file an information, is a right of prerogative" traceable to the powers of the king as *parens patriae* "to see that right is done to his subjects who are

---

[127] *Id.* at 47, 49.

[128] 30 Va. (3 Leigh) 690 (1832).

[129] *Id.* at 701.

[130] *Id. Accord*, Hathaway v. Village of New Baltimore, 48 Mich. 251, 254, 12 N.W. 186, 187 (1882).

[131] 43 U.S. (2 How.) 127, 195 (1844). *Accord*, 2 Kent's Commentaries, *supra* note 21, at *287-88.

incompetent to act for themselves, as in the case of charities. . . . "[132]
If the role of the Crown and the attorney general in the enforcement
of charitable trusts was a right of prerogative, as Story's opinion asserts, then the attorney general would have no function whatever in
the enforcement or supervision of charitable trusts, since it was well
understood that the royal prerogative rights were not adopted in the
new nation.[133] That outcome would be perfectly consistent with the
holding in *Vidal*, since that was a suit by heirs against the executor;
the attorney general was not even a party. The traditional function
performed by the English attorney general—filing an information
in equity to declare the validity of a charitable trust—could therefore
be performed by private litigants.

Whatever the merit of the suggestion that the chancellor had
common-law enforcement powers but the attorney general did not,
it reached its apogee in 1844 with the *Vidal* decision and was then
nudged toward obscurity by Chief Justice Shaw in *Parker v. May*.[134]
In *Parker* the commonwealth attorney had brought an information
in the nature of a bill in equity to challenge alleged misappropriations
of charitable property. Though dismissing the bill on its merits, for
reasons to be discussed under the subsection on charitable corporations, Shaw conceded that "[t]he power to institute and prosecute a
suit of this nature, in order to establish and carry into effect an important branch of the public interest," was "a common-law power,
incident to the office of attorney-general. . . . "[135] That dictum has
since been accepted as a leading statement of the attorney general's
common-law powers.

---

[132] 43 U.S. (2 How.) at 195 (quoting Attorney-General v. Mayor of Dublin, 4 Eng. Rep. 888, 902 (Ch. 1827)).

[133] *See* authorities cited at note 41 *supra*.

[134] 59 Mass. (5 Cush.) 336 (1850).

[135] *Id*. at 338. This is said to be the first American decision on the common-law powers of the attorney general. NATIONAL ASSOCIATION OF AT-
TORNEYS GENERAL, THE OFFICE OF THE ATTORNEY GENERAL 33 (1971).
The other aspects of the case are discussed in text accompanying notes 178-
84 *infra*.

The attorney general's power to "enforce" charitable *trusts* is now well recognized, although the extent of authority conferred by that ambiguous term is still undefined. Since a charitable trust is for the general benefit of the public or some numerically significant segment of it, there are no identifiable beneficiaries to perform the enforcement functions that extend beyond the threshold "establishment" of its validity.[136] If any individual member of the public could bring suit to challenge the administration of a charitable trust, the trust could be depleted by vexatious and expensive litigation. As a result, it is best to have a public officer perform the needed enforcement functions.

> Since the Attorney General is the governmental officer whose duties include the protection of the rights of the people of the state in general, it is natural that he has been chosen as the protector, supervisor, and enforcer of charitable trusts, both in England and in the several states, either because of a specific delegation of that power to him by statute, or by reason of a general statement of his duties, or because of judicial precedent.[137]

The attorney general may proceed on his own initiative, or at the request of some interested citizen, called the "relator," who has brought an alleged irregularity to the attention of the attorney general and demanded action.[138] As Bogert indicates, the sources of the attorney general's power to enforce charitable trusts are sometimes statutory, sometimes a general statement of duties, and sometimes judicial precedent declaring him to have succeeded to the common-

---

[136] The trustee named by the settlor or another appointed under the inherent powers of equity can provide the initial enforcement function of establishing the validity of a charitable trust. The heirs of the settlor, who have an incentive to challenge the validity of the trust, should provide an adversary consideration of this question. *See also* text accompanying note 133 *supra*.

[137] G. BOGERT, *supra* note 27 § 411. *Accord*, 4 A. SCOTT, *supra* note 20 § 391; C. ZOLLMAN, *supra* note 26, §§ 613-617.

[138] G. BOGERT, *supra* note 27, § 411.

law powers of the English attorney general.[139] But while the requisite power "to enforce" seems to be universally recognized, the critical inquiry in current times is not the existence or source of the power but its extent.

An inquiry into the extent of the attorney general's common-law enforcement power is hampered by the paucity of court decisions. "While statements that the attorney general has a common-law power to supervise charities are abundant," the leading treatise on charities declares, "cases involving the exercise of this power are rare."[140] The authorities are summarized below.

One large category of cases involving the common-law "enforcement" powers of the attorney general deals with that officer's duty to *establish and defend* the validity of charitable trusts. As already noted, the attorney general's earliest enforcement duty with respect to charitable trusts was to bring an information in the court of chancery to obtain a decree establishing their validity.[141] Although that duty may have involved a prerogative power of the chancellor in the beginning, it survives as an accepted judicial function of the court of equity and an acknowledged common-law power of the attorney general in

---

[139] *E.g.*, Estate of Pruner v. Hayes, 390 Pa. 529, 531, 136 A.2d 107, 109 (1957) ("The responsibility for public supervision traditionally has been delegated to the attorney general to be performed as an exercise of his *parens patriae* powers."); Sarkeys v. Independent School Dist. No. 40, 592 P.2d 529 (Okla. 1979); State v. Taylor, 58 Wash. 2d 252, 362 P.2d 247 (1961). *Contra*, Hedin v.. Westdala Lutheran Church, 59 Idaho 241, 81 P.2d 741 (1938) (attorney general has no common-law power to enforce charitable trusts—decision now reversed by statute, Dolan v. Johnson, 95 Idaho 385, 509 P.2d 1306 (1973); Powers v. First Nat'l Bank of Corsicana, 138 Tex. 604, 161 S.W.2d 273 (1942) (no English common-law enforcement powers in state attorney general); Estate of Sharp v. State, 63 Wis. 2d 254, 217 N.W.2d 258 (1974) (attorney general has no *parens patriae* powers). *See generally* NA-TIONAL ASSOCIATION OF ATTORNEYS GENERAL, COMMON LAW POWERS OF ATTORNEYS GENERAL 1 37-38, 43-45 (rev. ed. 1977); NATIONAL ASSOCIATION OF ATTORNEYS GENERAL, *supra* note 135, at 32-61.

[140] E. FISCH, D. FREED & E. SCHACHTER, *supra* note 19, § 682.

[141]. *See* text accompanying note 34 *supra*.

that officer's duty to defend charitable trusts against attacks on their validity or attempts to terminate them by the heirs of the donor.[142]

Almost all of the other common-law cases of attorney general participation in litigation over charitable trusts involve what might be called *responsive representation*, where the attorney general performs a relatively routine representative role, most often at the initiative of the trustees and usually not adverse to them. This category would include cases in which the attorney general participates in litigation proposing an alteration of the charitable activity by cy pres,[143] or in which he serves as a formal party in litigation brought to achieve some lesser administrative objective such as substituting trustees[144] or constructing the meaning of the trust instrument.[145]

The final category of "enforcement" involves the *breach of trust*, such as when it is alleged that the trustee of a charitable trust has diverted trust assets to personal use or a use outside the prescribed charitable purpose, or has been guilty of making improper investments or other administrative actions not conforming to the re-

---

[142] *E.g., In re* Powers' Estate, 362 Mich. 222, 106 N.W.2d 833 (1961); Estate of Pruner v. Hayes, 390 Pa. 529, 136 A.2d 107 (1957); Estate of Goodrich v. Union Trust Co., 271 Wis. 59, 72 N.W.2d 698 (1955); G. Bogert, *supra* note 27 § 411 & nn.23, 33-34; 4 A. Scott,*supra* note 20 § 391 nn.3, 16. The ground of invalidity can be mortmain legislation, perpetuities, absence of requisite formalities, undue influence, etc.

[143] *E.g., In re* Owens' Estate, 244 Iowa 533, 57 N.W.2d 193 (1953); Crow v. Clay County, 196 Mo. 234, 95 S.W. 369 (1906); Concord Nat'l Bank v. Town of Haverhill, 101 N.H. 416, 145 A.2d 61 (1958); Commonwealth v. Pauline Home, 141 Pa. 537, 21 A. 661 (1891); cases cited in G. Bogert,*supra* note 27, § 411, at 415 n.23; cases cited at note 267 *infra*.

[144] *E.g.,* State v. Bibb, 234 Ala. 46, 173 So. 74 (1937); *In re* Wilson, 372 Mass. 325, 361 N.E.2d 1281 (1977); *In re* Grblny's Estate, 147 Nev. 117, 22 N.W.2d 488 (1946), *overruled on other grounds*, Anoka-Butte Lumber Co. v. Malerbi, 180 Neb. 256, 142 N.W.2d 314 (1966).

[145] *E.g.,* Copp v. Barnum, 160 Conn. 557, 276 A.2d 893 (1970); Bishop v. Kemp, 35 Hawaii 1 (1939); Leo v. Armington, 74 R.I. 124, 59 A.2d 371 (1948); Finger v. School Sisters of Third Order of St. Francis, 585 S.W.2d 357 (Tex. Civ. App. 1979); G. Bogert,*supra* note 27, § 411, at 415 n.23, 424 n.33; 4 A. Scott,*supra* note 20, § 391, at 3007 n.16.

quired standard of care. Unlike the instances of responsive representation discussed above, this category always requires the initiative of the attorney general, and it is inevitably adverse to the trustees. Although there are many statements in the cases and treatises to the effect that the attorney general has this kind of enforcement power, actual common-law holdings to this effect are extremely rare. Most of the judicial opinions on this subject are dicta on the facts of the case[146] or represent statements with at least partial reliance on statutory rather than common-law authority.[147] The widespread adoption of legislation empowering the attorney general to enforce and supervise charitable trusts, discussed in the next part, is persuasive evidence of the inadequacy or ambiguity of common-law powers in this area.

In this circumstance it is not possible to confirm the attorney general's common-law enforcement power to challenge breaches of trust in charitable trusts generally, but it would be risky to deny it entirely.[148] What can be said with certainty is that the author has been unable to find any case outside California in which the attorney general has initiated breach of trust litigation against the trustees of a functioning *church* or in which a court has issued an opinion holding that the attorney general has common-law enforcement powers over

---

[146] *E.g.*, People v. Cogswell, 113 Cal. 129, 45 P. 270 (1896) (issue on appeal was validity; mismanagement allegations settled by stipulation), discussed in text accompanying note 243 *infra*; People *ex rel.* Smith v. Braucher, 258 Ill. 604, 101 N.E. 944 (1913) (bill dismissed).

[147] *E.g.*, Israel v. National Bd. of Y.M.C.A., 369 A.2d 646 (R.I. 1977); People v. George F. Harding Museum, 58 Ill. App. 3d 408, 374 N.E.2d 756 (1978).

[148] Compare the attorney general's initiative powers under quo warranto, text accompanying note 173 *infra*, and the discussion of his other powers with respect to charitable corporations, text accompanying notes 178-90 *infra*. *But cf.* People *ex rel.* Smith v. Braucher, 258 Ill. 604, 101 N.E. 944 (1913) (bill to set aside sale of real estate by trustees of incorporated religious society that had been defunct for 20 years dismissed on merits because of inapplicability of cy pres); authorities cited at note 149 *infra*.

church officers or trustees on the basis that they are the trustees of a charitable trust.[149]

References to the common-law "superintending" or "supervisory" functions of the attorney general or jurisdiction of the court of equity seem to imply another category of enforcement powers, which could be called *investigatory and supervisory*. Does the common-law authority to "enforce" charitable trusts include any authority to investigate and supervise the administration of charitable trusts in general, such as by requiring regular reports or by reviewing the trustee's decisions in the administration of the trust? Judicial pronouncements on that subject are also sparse, being limited to a handful of cases dealing with unusual factual circumstances whose holdings offer no authority for the assertion of a general common-law authority of this nature.

Commonwealth v. Barnes Foundation[150] involved a foundation established to maintain an art gallery open to the public. When it appeared that the trustees refused admission to the public, the Pennsyvlania attorney general obtained an order compelling the trustees to show cause why they should not open the gallery to the public, and sought discovery of the books and records of the foundation necessary to pursue the litigation. Noting the attorney general's duty to ascertain the facts surrounding an activity that enjoyed tax exemption and recognizing his common-law powers "to inquire into the status, activities and functioning of public charities," the Pennsylvania Supreme Court held that the trustees should answer the show cause order and that the attorney general should have "suit-

---

[149] *But see* Chambers v. Baptist Educ. Soc'y, 40 Ky. (1 B. Mon.) 215 (1841) (dictum that attorney general has common-law and statutory power to bring chancery suit to challenge diversion of funds in charitable trust to educate Baptist ministers); MacKenzie v. Trustees of Presbytery of Jersey City, 67 N.J. Eq. 652, 683-86 (1905) (heirs of donor of real estate to church had no standing to enjoin trustees against diverting trust property to a charitable use not specified in original gift because, court declared, only attorney general or church's representative could properly invoke court's superintending power over charitable trusts).

[150] 398 Pa. 458, 467, 159 A.2d 500, 505-06 (1960).

able discovery" incident thereto. This case affirms the attorney general's power to bring suit to compel a charitable trustee to go forward with the performance of the charitable activity—a ruling analogous to a declaration of the validity of the charity—but the discovery aspect of the holding offers no precedent for imposing a duty to make routine periodic reports. In contrast, the New York Appellate Division, in an earlier decision, held that the attorney general could not compel the trustees to submit a plan of distribution of charitable funds when there was no showing that the trustee was performing his duties improperly."[151]

In *State v. Taylor*[152] the Washington attorney general brought an accounting proceeding against trustees who had refused to respond to his request that they provide him extensive information on the trust, including property, income, disbursements, and all legal actions and changes in trust administration. The supreme court held that the trial court had properly dismissed the complaint because the attorney general had asked for too much information. The court mentioned the common-law powers of the attorney general and referred to what it called the substantially identical duties of the trustees of private and charitable trusts to keep records, respond to a judicially administered accounting, and provide the beneficiary, on request, with "*all information about the trust and its execution for which he has any reasonable use.*" The court continued as follows:

> We conclude on the basis of the foregoing reasoning and authority, as a general proposition, that the Attorney General, as representative of the public and particularly of those individuals who may be specially benefited, has standing to maintain an action against the trustees of a charitable trust to obtain information concerning the course of administration, provided that the demand is not unreasonable in view of the circumstances and nature and status of the particular trust.

---

[151] Buell v. Gardner, 16 Misc. 116, 149 N.Y.S. 803 (Sup. Ct. 1914), *aff'd*, 168 A.D. 278, 153 N.Y.S. 1108 (1915). G. BOGERT, *supra* note 27, § 411, states, "But in the absence of statute [the attorney general] cannot compel the trustees to submit to him their plans for administration of the charity, when there is no allegation of actual or threatened breach and no doubt as to the intent of the settlor."

[152] 58 Wash. 2d 252, 362 P.2d 247 (1961).

> ... While we can appreciate the interest and efforts of the Attorney General of Washington relative to effective enforcement of the duties and responsibilities of trustees of charitable trusts in this state, we must conclude that in the absence of statutory authorization he cannot require of the charitable trustees the continuing communication of information and unreasonable duplication of records and information instanced by the letter of demand. The Attorney General's power to enforce charitable trusts is coextensive with, but no broader than, the power of enforcement enjoyed by beneficiaries of private trusts.[153]

This is the fragmentary state of the attorney general's common-law authority to exercise "supervisory" jurisdiction over the management of trusts.

Consistent with the rationale that the attorney general enforces a charitable trust in the absence of any other identifiable beneficiary who can perform this function, there are circumstances in which this officer has been denied any enforcement role whatever. In *Attorney General v. Clark*[154] the attorney general, on the relation of church trustees, filed an information to compel the trustees of the Twelfth Baptist Building Association, which had obtained contributions for the repair of the church building, to apply the funds for that purpose. A decree dismissing the information was affirmed. The court explained: "While equity will enforce a valid trust, charitable or otherwise, it does not do so upon an information filed by the attorney general, if the trust is in effect a private one. . . . "[155] The court said that the attorney general's enforcement role in charitable trusts was limited to what the court called "a public charity," in which "those who are entitled to the benefit of the donation are incapable of asserting their own right."[156] In this case, on the other hand, the trust was in effect a private one because "the Twelfth Baptist Church is a definite body, capable of enforcing whatever rights it may have in the

---

[153] *Id.* at 260-61, 264, 362 P.2d at 252, 254.

[154] 167 Mass. 201, 45 N.E. 183 (1896).

[155] *Id.* at 203, 45 N.E. at 184.

[156] *Id.* at 204, 45 N.E. at 184.

fund in controversy."[157] As a result, the attorney general had no role in the trust's enforcement.[158] This principle, which is sustained in the treatises and in a holding on corporate charities,[159] is apparently applicable to a wide variety of circumstances, including some involving churches, in which there are entities or constituencies with legal capacity and sufficient interest to see that a charitable trust is enforced without the involvement of the attorney general.[160]

It appears from the foregoing that in the United States the attorney general's common-law power to "enforce" charitable trusts clearly includes the right to bring suits to establish and defend the validity of the trust and to be involved in what is here called "respon-

---

[157] Id.

[158] Id. Accord, Parker v. May, 59 Mass (5 Cush.) 336, 348, 351-52 (1850). The public-private distinction has also been used to describe the difference between a valid and an invalid charitable trust. E.g., C. ZOLLMAN, supra note 26, §§ 204-205, 353.

[159] Lefkowitz v. Lebensfeld, 51 N.Y.2d 442, 415 N.E.2d 919 (1980) (attorney general without standing to enforce property rights of charitable corporation in behalf of its beneficiaries); 2 J. PERRY, supra note 41, § 732; G. BOGERT, supra note 27, § 414; 4 A. SCOTT, supra note 20, § 391. 3 J. STORY, supra note 31, § 1546, suggests that this category of charitable trust "for a definite object, and the trustee living" was the first kind of charitable trust the equity court enforced by an original bill independent of the jurisdiction conferred by the Statute of Charitable Uses.

[160] E.g., Sunday School Union of African Methodist Episcopal Church v. Walden, 121 F.2d 719 (6th Cir. 1941); Stern v. Lucy Webb Hanes Nat'l Training School for Deaconesses and Missionaries, 367 F. Supp. 536 (D.D.C. 1973); Jones v. Grant, 344 So. 2d 1210 (Ala. 1977); Pratt v. Security Trust & Sav. Bank, 15 Cal. App. 2d 630, 59 P.2d 862 (1936); Paterson v. Paterson Gen. Hosp., 97 N.J. Super. 514, 235 A.2d 487 (1967); authorities cited at note 159 supra. Cf. Cocke v. Duke Univ., 260 N.C. 1, 131 S.E.2d 909 (1963) (trustee has authority to select charitable organizations to receive trust income; possible recipients can enforce trust by class action); Ware v. Cumberlege, 52 Eng. Rep. 697 (M.R. 1855) (attorney general need not be party to suit challenging validity of testamentary dispositions to "specified individual charities" which can represent their own interests). The so-called subtrustee can maintain a suit to enforce the trust against the primary trustee without joining the attorney general. G. BOGERT, supra note 27 § 413 n.53.

sive representation," including suits to construe the trust instrument, to replace trustees, and to alter the trust purpose by cy pres. The attorney general's common-law power to bring suit against charitable trustees for breach of trust is the subject of announcement in the treatises and dicta in the cases, but is not well established by court holdings and is unheard of outside of California in the case of religious uses of church properties allegedly held in trust. Court decisions on the attorney general's "supervisory" authority to require regular reports or to review the trustee's management of the trust are sparse, conflicting, and so narrowly reasoned as to provide no support for the general existence of such a power. The statutes on this last subject, enacted because of the apparent absence of common-law authority, are discussed in Part IV. Finally, in those circumstances in which the charitable trust had an identifiable beneficiary capable of enforcing the beneficial rights in the charitable trust, such as a church or other corporation for which the property was held, some decisions denied the attorney general any enforcement role whatever.

3. The charitable corporation

With respect to charitable corporations, the attorney general's common-law enforcement powers are far more tenuous than for charitable trusts. Unlike the situation with individual charitable trustees, in which the attorney general may be needed to fill a void in enforcement, a charitable corporation has built-in enforcement opportunities and responsibilities that make the attorney general's intervention far less necessary. This is why, as noted earlier, the English courts of equity and attorney general had no enforcement functions with respect to the administration of corporate charities. After reviewing two legal remedies unique to corporations—the role and significance of the "visitors" of charitable corporations and the remedy of quo warranto—this subsection will review the common-law principles that have restricted the jurisdiction of the equity court and the attorney general in the enforcement or supervision of charitable corporations, especially those chartered for a religious purpose.

a. Visitorial powers. The earliest American common-law decisions on the attorney general's supervisory authority over charitable corporations involved his visitorial power over charitable eleemosynary corporations, including churches, hospitals, schools, and colleges.[161] In a leading decision in 1817, Chancellor Kent rejected the New York attorney general's attempt to use "the power of visitation and superintending the conduct of corporations" as a basis for enjoining a business corporation from unauthorized banking operations. The visitorial power, which devolved upon the King when he was the founder of a charity or when the founder had not appointed other visitors, applied only to *charitable* corporations. As to these, the learned chancellor added an important dictum. When the English chancellor or the courts of law exercised visitorial powers over charitable institutions, they had done so as the personal representatives of the Crown, not as judicial officers. Consequently, Kent concluded, "I doubt much whether the visitorial power exists at all, and in any case in this court, in the English sense of that power, as a right emanating from the royal prerogative and founded on discretion."[162] An aggrieved party had other remedies. The charitable corporation was amenable in a court of law for misuse of its corporate franchise, and its officers "may, in their character of trustees, be accountable to this [equity] court for a fraudulent breach of trust."[163]

In the celebrated *Dartmouth College* case,[164] the United States Supreme Court held that the constitutional prohibition against impairing the obligation of contracts prohibited a state from materially altering the crown charter incorporating a Christian college established by private donations. Chief Justice Marshall's opinion rejected the contention that this "private eleemosynary" corporation was a charitable trust for the people of New Hampshire, which would have made it subject to general oversight by an equity court. Instead, he

---

[161] *See generally* 2 KENT'S COMMENTARIES, *supra* note 21, at *300-04.

[162] Attorney-General v. Utica Ins. Co., 2 Johns. Ch. 412, 420 (N.Y. Ch. 1817). The reporter's note adds, "But whether ecclesiastical, eleemosynary, or civil, our court of chancery has no jurisdiction as visitor over religious corporations." *Id.* at 414 n.

[163] *Id.* at 420. Under this heading the court cited diversion of funds for personal use or for business beyond the authorized corporate purpose.

[164] Trustees of Dartmouth College v. Woodward, 17 U.S (4 Wheat.) 518, 524 (1819).

held that the corporation possessed "the whole legal and equitable interest."[165] Justice Joseph Story's opinion did not disagree with that conclusion, but went on to describe the visitorial power,[166] concluding that "[w]hen a private eleemosynary corporation is thus created by the charter of the crown, it is subject to no other control on the part of the crown, than what is expressly or implicitly reserved by the charter itself." However, Story qualified this principle by suggesting that the "trustees" of a corporate charity were "subject to the general superintending power of the Court of Chancery . . . in all cases of an abuse of trusts to redress grievances, and suppress frauds."[167]

Story's hint that the "trustees" of a charitable corporation might be subject to judicial supervision, nothwithstanding the English view that the visitorial powers derived equity of jurisdiction,[168] was later

---

[165] *Id.* at 654.

[166] The visitorial power was attached to all eleemosynary corporations and was exercised by the founder and his heirs, as "a power to visit, inquire into, and correct all irregularities and abuses in such corporations, and to compel the original purposes of the charity to be faithfully fulfilled." *Id.* at 673.

[167] *Id.* at 675-76. "And where a corporation is a mere trustee of a charity, a Court of equity will go yet farther; and though it cannot appoint or remove a corporator, it will yet, in a case of gross fraud, or abuse of trust, take away the trust from the corporation, and vest it in other hands." *Id.* at 676-77. Justice Story elaborated on the "visitorial power" in Allen v. McKean, 1 Fed. Cas. 489 (C.C. Me. 1833) (No. 229), characterizing it as "a necessary incident to all eleemosynary corporations," and as a "mere power to control and arrest abuses, and to enforce a due observance of the statutes of the charity. . . . [Where] *trustees* are incorporated to manage [a] charity, the visitorial power is deemed to belong to such trustee in their corporate capacity." *Id.* at 497-98. In that event, Story held,

> there can be . . . no disturbance or interference with the just exercise of their authority, unless it is reserved by the statutes of the foundation or charter. But, still, as managers of the revenues of the charity, they are not beyond control; but are subject to the general superintendence of a court of chancery, for any abuse of their trust in the management of it.

Id. at 498.

[168] *See* text accompanying note 50 *supra*.

confirmed by Chief Justice Lemuel Shaw, one of our greatest common-law judges, in a leading opinion which explained the relative
functions of the trustees, the visitors, and the court in a charitable corporation. In *Nelson v. Cushing*,[169] decided in 1848, the officer exercising the attorney general's powers in Massachusetts filed an
information to restrain incorporated trustees of a school established
"for the instruction of youth" from educating girls as well as boys.
The bill was dismissed on the merits because "youth" included both
sexes and also because the complainant's first recourse should have
been to the visitors designated by the settlor. Chief Justice Shaw
explained:

> The trustees and the visitors taken together, each acting in their own
> sphere, constitute the regular government of the charitable institu-
> tion; and, until they have finally acted, and acted contrary to law and
> in violation of their trust, no such breach can be held to exist. But the
> powers of this court, under its general jurisdiction in equity over
> trusts, when properly applied to, may be invoked to prevent or re-
> dress a breach of trust, arising from a misapplication of funds placed
> in trust for charitable purposes.[170]

Thus, the equity court had powers over a charitable corporation, notwithstanding the visitorial powers, but only as to "a misapplication of
funds placed in trust." The question of whether a charitable corporation held its assets "in trust" when no express trust had been created
is discussed below.[171]

It was perhaps inevitable that the visitor's authority would turn
out to be largely theoretical in a country whose institutions were not
friendly toward the essentially aristocratic hereditary visitorial rights
of the heirs of the donor. In any case, for one reason or another, vis-

---

[169] 56 Mass. (2 Cush.) 519 (1848).

[170] *Id.* at 532. *Accord*, Parker v. May, 59 Mass. (5 Cush.) 336 (1850), *quoted in* text accompanying note 182 *infra*; 2 J. PERRY, *supra* note 41, § 742; 2 KENT'S COMMENTARIES, *supra* note 21, at *304.

[171] *See* text accompanying notes 178-205 *infra*.

itorial powers have been used only rarely in the United States.[172] Under the modern law they obviously provide neither a court of equity nor the attorney general any authority for the exercise of supervisory powers as the successor of the residual visitorial powers of the Crown, and they have not been a barrier to the exercise of whatever enforcement or supervisory authority the law may otherwise grant to a court of equity or the attorney general with respect to charitable corporations.

b. Quo warranto. Another remedy unique to the corporate form of charity is the action or writ of quo warranto. As with other corporations, a corporate charity can exercise only the powers conferred by its charter. Quo warranto is the remedy for prohibiting a corporation from misusing or exceeding its charter powers.[173] The right to pursue this remedy was one of the attorney general's common-law powers generally recognized in this country.[174] By this means, a court

---

[172] Visitorial powers only apply to the original gift to the corporation and not to any new gifts. 2 J. PERRY, *supra* note 41, § 743. Even where clearly reserved, the visitorial powers have been held to have been delegated to others than the settlor or his heirs or to have been suspended in favor of the "superintending powers of [the] court[s]." MacKenzie v. Trustees of Presbytery of Jersey City, 67 N.J. Eq. 652, 678, 680-83 (1905); E. FISCH, D. FREED & E. SCHACHTER, *supra* note 19, § 681. For more modern cases on the visitorial power, *see e.g.,* Sarkeys v. Independent School Dist. No. 40, 592 P.2d 529, 535 (Okla. 1979) (visitors' appeal dismissed; right of visitation deemed a "relic"); State v. Taylor, 58 Wash. 2d 252, 362 p.2d 247 (1961) (visitation rights don't preclude attorney general initiatives); Trustees of Putnam Free School v. Attorney General, 320 Mass. 94, 67 N.E.2d 658 (1946) (filling vacancies in the visitors whom the trust instrument empowered to select trustees and supervise investments and application of income). *See generally* G. BOGERT, *supra* note 27, § 416; 4 A. SCOTT, *supra* note 20, § 391; E. FISCH, D. FREED & E. SHACHTER, *supra* note 19, §§ 680-681; C. ZOLLMAN, *supra* note 26, §§ 603-610.

[173] 7 S. THOMPSON, COMMENTARIES ON THE LAW OF CORPORATIONS, §§ 5780-5811, esp. § 5783 (3d ed. White 1927); 5 W. FLETCHER, CYCLOPEDIA OF THE LAW OF PRIVATE CORPORATIONS § 2332 (rev. perm. ed. 1975); Comment, *Quo Warranto in Pennsylvania: Old Standards and New Developments*, 80 DICK. L. REV. 218, 237-44 (1975).

[174] 7 S. THOMPSON, *supra* note 173, § 5792; NATIONAL ASSOCIATION OF ATTORNEYS GENERAL, *supra* note 139, at 39-41.

could compel the officers and directors of a charitable corporation to abide by the provisions of their corporate charter, revoking the charter if they did not.[175]

The quo warranto power was even available to revoke the charter of a church corporation, or to use against persons "usurping the franchises and privileges of the governing board of an incorporated church association."[176] Thus, in a Pennsylvania case the attorney general brought an action of quo warranto against a church incorporated in 1814 which had no more members and which had ceased to function as a religious organization. He alleged that the corporate officers had wilfully violated and exceeded the charter powers, wasted corporate property, and failed to exercise the charter privileges. A judgment forfeiting the corporate charter was affirmed on appeal, the court declaring:

> The facts recited above disclose a long record of flagrant violation of the provisions of the corporate charter; the corporation has disregarded the purposes for which it was created, it has violated the condition upon which it was enabled to acquire and hold property, it has exercised its corporate charter to administer a charitable use for the private gain or benefit of its trustees, and there has been supine neglect to remedy the situation.[177]

The power to insist that a charitable corporation operate within the activities authorized by its corporate charter is, of course, a far less

---

[175] E.g., People v. Milk Producers' Ass'n of Central California, Inc., 60 Cal. App. 439, 212 P. 957 (1923); Miami Retreat Foundation v. Ervin, 62 S. 2d 748 (Fla. 1952); Commonwealth v. Seventh Day Baptists of Ephrata, 317 Pa. 358, 361, 176 A. 17, 19 (1935); G. BOGERT, supra note 27 § 411, at 415, and § 416, at 455-56; NATIONAL ASSOCIATION OF STATE ATTORNEYS GENERAL, COMMON LAW POWERS OF STATE ATTORNEYS GENERAL 46-47 (rev. ed. 1977).

[176] 7 S. THOMPSON, supra note 173, § 5785. Accord, State v. Minimum Salary Dep't of African Methodist Episcopal Church, Inc., 447 S.W.2d 11 (Tenn. 1972) (diversion of funds). Quo warranto was not, however, the correct remedy to challenge the authority of ministers of churches since they were not regarded as public officers or exercising public office or franchise. Id.; 5 W. FLETCHER, supra note 173 § 2332 nn.17-19.

[177] Commonwealth v. Seventh Day Baptists of Ephrata, 317 Pa. 358, 361, 176 A. 17, 19 (1935).

extensive power than is suggested by the "supervision" or even the "enforcement" of a charitable trust, but it is a power well suited to the special circumstances of the corporate form of organization, and especially to the limited official involvement appropriate for the charitable activities undertaken by religious charitable corporations.

    c. Enforcement or supervisory authority over corporations. Apart from the special remedy of quo warranto and the special implications of the visitorial authority, what, if any, enforcement or supervisory authority did a court of equity or the attorney general have over charitable corporations, especially those organized for religious purposes? Did such corporations hold their assets in trust, subject to judicial enforcement like charitable trustees, or were they autonomous in their management like other corporations? The earliest leading opinion on those questions is, again, that of the gifted Chief Justice Shaw. In *Parker v. May*,[178] decided in 1850, the commonwealth attorney had brought an information in the nature of a bill in equity against a legislatively-chartered church corporation and its trustees. He sought to prevent what he called a misapplication of contributed funds "to other than the charitable uses for which the same were alleged to be appropriated," specifically, a large payment to a former pastor as an expression of confidence and respect. Shaw had heard the case in chancery and rendered an opinion later concurred in unanimously by the Supreme Judicial Court.

    The chief justice distinguished between the voluntary association of "the church," consisting of the members who would gather from time to time, and the "incorporated religious society," a perpetual identity in the person of the deacons, which held the property.[179] The commonwealth attorney was apparently relying on the doctrine of implied trust to argue that the corporation held the property in a charitable trust for the members of the church, which would of course give him a common-law basis for seeking relief to enforce the trust. Although conceding that the attorney general had a common-

---

[178] 59 Mass. (5 Cush.) 336 (1850).

[179] *Id.* at 344-45.

law power to "prosecute a suit of this nature,"[180] Shaw held that the attorney general's enforcement power did not apply to every case of "property or funds held for purposes of charity."[181] That power did not reach this case because here the property was held by the corporation and not in trust:

> The church and the deacons together, therefore, take and hold the property in their own right, with a full and unlimited power of disposition, subject to no trust, and especially subject to no trust for general charity, which would render them amenable to this court, upon an information in equity by the public prosecutor.[182]

Even if the corporate property were regarded as held in trust for the members or religious purposes of the church, the suit still could not be maintained because the court's supervisory authority did not extend to this church corporation. "A church, recognized as a body having power to administer its funds for particular purposes . . . resemble[s] . . . a body constituted by charter to administer charitable relief," and "[t]he controlling power of the court over charities does not extend to a charity regulated by governors under a charter, unless they abuse their trust in regard to the revenues."[183]

Consequently, the remedy was for the church organization to remove the deacons and appoint others. "In this way," the chief justice declared, "any breach of their trust by the deacons, to the injury of the church, may be prevented or redressed without the aid of the commonwealth [attorney]."[184]

In another leading case, *Robertson v. Bullions*,[185] decided in 1854, the New York Court of Appeals also rejected the argument that the legislative act incorporating a church had the effect of incorporating

---

[180] *Id.* at 338, discussed in text accompanying notes 134-35 *supra.*

[181] *Id.* at 341.

[182] *Id.* at 350. *See also id.* at 348-51. The public prosecutor exercised the attorney general's powers at this time in Massachusetts. *Id.* at 338.

[183] *Id.* at 351.

[184] *Id.* at 352. For a discussion of the religious atmosphere in which this case was decided, see L. LEVY, *supra* note 86.

[185] 11 N.Y. 243 (1854), discussed in text at notes 93-97 *supra.*

the church "trustees," who then held the corporate property in charitable trust for the members and purposes of the church. The court's reasoning is very significant:

> Were this [trust] view established, its effect would probably be, to devolve upon the courts of equity the administration of the entire property of religious corporations throughout the state, a jurisdiction bringing with it as its inevitable concomitant, enumerable judicial inquiries into modes of faith, shades of religious opinion, and all those subtleties which attend the diversities of religious belief.[186]

Instead, the court held that the entire society was deemed incorporated, with the voluntary association of church members "merged in the corporation, so far as its secular affairs merely are concerned," and with the trustees "clothed with the customary discretionary powers which appertain to the managing officers of all civil corporations; modified it is true in some degree, by . . . the peculiar object of the incorporation."[187] The court ruled, further, that

> [T]hese incorporated societies are not to be regarded as ecclesiastical corporations, in the sense of the English law, which were composed entirely of ecclesiastical persons, and subject to the ecclesiastical judicatories; but as belonging to the class of civil corporations to be controlled and managed according to the principles of the common law, as administered by the ordinary tribunals of justice.[188]

---

[186] *Id.* at 247.

[187] *Id.* at 247-48. *See generally* Kauper & Ellis, *supra* note 94.

[188] 11 N.Y. at 251-52. The court then referred to Chancellor Kent's opinion in Attorney-General v. Utica Ins. Co., 2 Johns. Ch. 412 (N.Y. Ch. 1817), discussed in text at note 162 *supra*, to the effect that, in Justice Selden's words,

> the court of chancery did not possess any general supervisory control over corporations of this character, and [Kent] inclined to the opinion that the court had no jurisdiction whatever, even in a case of abuse by a corporate trustee, or other officer of his trust, by a perversion of misapplication of the funds of the corporation.

11 N.Y. at 252. Of course if a corporation were "made a trustee, having no beneficial interest in the fund," and if it "grossly abuses the trust, it will be removed by the court of chancery, in the same manner as an individual trustee." *Id.* at 253.

Robertson v. Bullions is a leading authority for the principle of corporate autonomy for charitable corporations[189] and a leading statement of the special importance of that autonomy in the case of church corporations.[190]

---

[189] Its leading status is evident from the use made of it in, *e.g.*, 1 THOMPSON, *supra* note 173, § 19; C. BOONE, A MANUAL OF THE LAW APPLICABLE TO CORPORATIONS § 270 (1887). According to Boone, a religious corporation is to be regarded as a civil corporation

> to be controlled and managed according to the principles of the common law. . . . [T]he trustees are but the managing officers of the corporation, invested, as to the temporal affairs of the society, with the powers specifically conferred by the statute, and with the ordinary discretionary powers of officers of civil corporations. . . . They are trustees in the same sense with the president and directors of a bank or of a railroad company.

Id.

[190] Contrary to suggestions in some cases rejecting its holdings (*e.g.*, Wheelock v. First Presbyterian Church 119 Cal. 477, 486, 51 P. 841, 845 (1897), discussed in text accompanying note 238 *infra*), *Robertson v. Bullions* does not seem to have been attributable to legal rules designed to accommodate New York's peculiar and short-lived rejection of the charitable trust, which forced all charitable dispositions into the corporate form if they were to be valid. The validity of the charitable trust was sustained in New York in Williams v. Williams, 8 N.Y. 525 (1853), against the contention that it had been eliminated by legislative action in 1788 and 1827. *See* text following note 123 *supra*. Decisions a few years later began to cast doubt on that holding, but it was not overruled even in part until Bascom v. Albertson, 34 N.Y. 584 (1866), and not totally rejected until Holmes v. Mead, 52 N.Y. 332 (1873). ZOLLMAN, *supra* note 118, at 101-02; Note, *supra* note 118, at 445-46. In that same year the court of appeals gave substantial impetus to the charitable corporation by ruling that a corporation created for charity could take a bequest without violating the rule against perpetuities. Even though the gift was limited to the use of the income, the corporation did not hold the gift in trust. Wetmore v. Parker, 52 N.Y. 450, 459 (1873). The continued validity of the rule in *Robertson v. Bullions* is evident from a recent case holding that the attorney general had no standing to represent the ultimate beneficiaries of a charitable corporation which was the donee of an unconditional gift of property, since the corporation did not hold the gift in trust. Lefkowitz v. Lebensfeld, 68 A.D.2d 488, 495-96, 417 N.Y.S.2d 715, 721 (1979), *aff'd*, 51 N.Y.2d 442, 415 N.E.2d 919 (1980).

4. Charitable trusts and corporations compared

The corporate autonomy doctrine propounded in *Parker v. May* and *Robertson v. Bullions* presupposes a far less comprehensive judicial enforcement or supervision mechanism for charitable corporations than for charitable trusts. The different circumstances of the two different forms of organization underline the appropriateness of that distinction, but when both trusts and corporations are involved in works of charity, there are also important similarities that should dictate similar legal treatment for many purposes. The number and relative economic importance of both types of charitable institutions enjoyed impressive growth in the second century of our national life, with accompanying increases in the complexity of the statutory and the common law by which these important institutions were governed. The remaining portion of this subsection will discuss significant interactions between the law of charitable trusts and charitable corporations.

The most important distinguishing characteristic of a corporate charity is that it is organized under legislative authority, either through individual charters or under general laws for the incorporation of nonprofit or charitable corporations. Legislative enactments generally make provision for the governance of corporations. Therefore, in contrast to a charitable trustee, who may be a sole trustee established by the private action of a single citizen, a charitable corporation must be established by a public act and within an organizational framework prescribed by law. Typically, that framework requires a significant number of corporate officers and directors or "trustees" who can serve as a check on one another. The legislation may also specify some reporting requirements. In addition, the kinds of functions performed by charitable corporations typically involve service to organized constituencies, such as church members, school students, or hospital patients, which also serve as a monitor and check on the activities of charitable corporations and their officers.

Despite the important differences between the charitable trust and the charitable corporation, these two types of charities have much in common, including rules of law representing concessions the law has made to the charitable trust that should be available to benefit all kinds of charitable enterprises regardless of their form of organization. The cy pres power is an example. This important equitable power to alter and save a frustrated charitable disposition should be available whether funds are held by a charitable trust or a charitable corporation. It is generally so held, as noted hereafter.[191] But the reasoning used in that holding is critical. If a court reasons that the cy pres power is only available for property held in a charitable *trust*, then the only way the court can use cy pres to save charitable property held by a corporation is to decree that a charitable corporation holds its property "in trust" for its charitable objects. So it is that in cy pres and a variety of analogous circumstances, courts have sometimes used the language of trust to justify decisions extending favored treatment to charitable corporations. But before applying the rhetoric of those decisions to different circumstances, such as to the attorney general's common-law enforcement and supervisory powers over charitable corporations, it is wise to look behind the labels to examine the facts of the cases in which the language was used.

It is, of course, clear at the outset that a charitable corporation can hold property as the trustee of an express charitable trust, even though the terms of the express trust are identical to some or all of the corporation's chartered purposes. If a settlor, with adequate formalities, communicated his intent that the grantee charitable corporation hold his donated property in trust, this would create an express charitable trust that could be enforced and administered just like any other charitable trust. In this manner, a church corporation can receive and administer an express charitable trust for the benefit of its missionary activities, its retired ministers, or its poor or aged members.[192] Such a trust is enforceable by a court of equity, with the attorney general having whatever enforcement and supervisory

---

[191] *See* text accompanying note 203 *infra*.

[192] King v. Richardson, 136 F.2d 849 (4th Cir. 1943) (missions); Ministers & Missionaries Benefit Bd. of Am. Baptist Convention v. Meriden Trust & Safe Deposit Co., 139 Conn. 435, 94 A.2d 917 (1953) (aged ministers); Roughton v. Jones, 225 Ga. 774, 171 S.E.2d 536 (1969) (missions); Hobbs v. Board of Educ. of Baptist Convention, 126 Neb. 416, 253 N.W. 627 (1934) (church endowment fund; only income usable for purposes of college);

powers that officer is granted by statutory or common law as to charitable trusts.

At the opposite extreme, if a donor makes an absolute gift to a charitable corporation, without any intent to create an express trust, there is no basis for charging the corporation with holding the property in trust unless the law imposes that consequence for some purposes, as discussed below. There is, as Bogert says, "a clear distinction" between this case and the case of an express trust:

> In the case of the *absolute gift* full ownership of the property given vests in the corporation, subject to the duties imposed upon it by its charter or articles of incorporation and by the terms of any agreements it makes by contract or its acceptance of a qualified gift. The Attorney General has the power, as a representative of the state and by quo warranto or other proceedings, to compel the corporation to perform these duties, but he acts in a different capacity than as enforcer of charitable trusts.[193]

As to the absolute gift, the attorney general's power is limited to ensuring that the charitable corporation stays within the powers granted by its corporate charter.

The difficult cases occur between these extremes, when a charitable corporation receives a gift with no evident intent to create an express trust, but with language limiting the use of the gift (or its income) to some designated portions of the corporation's activities. Bogert and Scott both cite a significant number of cases that divert from the traditional "absolute gift" rationale and use trust language in this situation, but both of these treatise writers conclude that even in these cases a statement that a charitable corporation holds its property in trust is subject to considerable qualification.

In Bogert's view the question turns on "whether the donor intended a trust or an absolute gift." He summarizes: "Under varying wordings of deeds and wills there has been a tendency to find an intent to give full title to the corporation, and not to make it a trustee,

---

General Ass'n of Davidian Seventh Day Adventists, Inc. v. General Ass'n of Davidian Seventh Day Adventists, 410 S.W.2d 256 (Tex. Civ. App. 1966) (old age assistance); *In re* Rowell's Estate, 248 Wis. 520, 22 N.W.2d 604 (1946) (care of poor).

[193] G. BOGERT, *supra* note 27, § 324.

but in some cases a trust intent has been found."[194] Under this interpretation, unless the individual donor clearly intended to create a trust, the corporation takes and holds the donor's gift without an enforceable restriction. Thus, the Supreme Court of Kansas ruled:

> Generally it has been held that where a gift is given to a corporation for the accomplishment of a purpose for which the corporation was formed, the gift is absolute and not in trust (69 C.J. 713), and more specifically, that where a gift is made to a religious or charitable corporation to aid in carrying out the purposes for which it was formed, it does not create a trust in any legal sense and is not to be judged by any of the well-known rules pertaining to the law of trusts as applied to individuals. 10 Am. Jur. 610.[195]

But, an approach that focuses on whether there was an absolute gift or a gift in trust implies the existence of substantive rules that dictate different consequences for a charitable corporation depending on which characterization is applied; as the Kansas court concludes, the trust rules do not apply to corporations. This may be true for certain rules, but it is clear from Bogert's treatise that for purposes of some rules embodying important concessions to and burdens on charities, such as the advantage of cy pres or the restrictions of mortmain, the rules are the same whether a corporation holds a restricted gift absolutely or in trust.[196] As a result, an approach that determines the inapplicability of other substantive rules to a charitable corporation by focusing on whether its property was acquired by a gift absolute or a gift in trust does not explain why that distinction governs the application of some substantive rules but not others.

Scott advocates a more promising approach to the middle ground. Focusing on the so-called "restricted gift" (limited to accom-

---

[194] *Id.* § 324, at 551 (footnote omitted).

[195] Zabel v. Stewart, 153 Kan. 272, 278-79, 109 P.2d 177, 181 (1941). *Accord, e.g.*, Sands v. Church of Ascension & Prince of Peace, 181 Md. 536, 30 A.2d 771 (1943); Y.W.C.A. v. Morgan, 281 N.C. 485, 189 S.E.2d 169 (1972); cases cited in G. BOGERT, *supra* note 27, § 324 n.13; 4 A. SCOTT, *supra* note 20, § 348.1 n.4; 5 W. PAGE ON THE LAW OF WILLS § 40.8, at 125 (Bowe-Parker rev. ed. 1960); C. ZOLLMAN, *supra* note 26, § 342. *But see id.* § 473.

[196] G. BOGERT, *supra* note 27, §§ 325-326 (mortmain legislation), § 431 (cy pres), § 352 (accumulations), § 264.25 (federal tax advantages).

plishing of one of the corporate purposes or limited to the use of income from the fund), Scott declares that "it cannot be stated dogmatically either that a charitable corporation is or that it is not a trustee." But he concludes that this uncertainty does not matter because "many of the principles applicable to charitable trusts are applicable to charitable corporations."[197] Similarly, the *Restatement (Second) of Trusts*, drafted by Scott, modifies the first *Restatement*'s position that a charitable corporation does not hold its gifts in trust[198] by calling the question "a mere matter of terminology." The second *Restatement* argues that the important question is "whether and to what extent the principles and rules applicable to charitable trusts are applicable to charitable corporations."[199]

Scott's reasoning is in harmony with the leading case of *St. Joseph's Hospital v. Bennett*,[200] in which the New York Court of Appeals held that an endowment gift to a hospital corporation with the income specified to be used "for the ordinary expenses of maintenance" could not be used to pay a mortgage debt. Although there was no trust "in a technical sense" and the "charitable corporation is not bound by all the limitations and rules which apply to a technical trustee," the court held that "equity will afford protection to a donor to a charitable corporation in that the Attorney-General may maintain a suit to compel the property to be held for the charitable purposes for which it was given to the corporation."[201] Similarly, a leading Pennsylvania decision held that a gift given to a Presbyterian

---

[197] A. SCOTT, *supra* note 20, § 348.1, at 2770-71, 2778.

[198] RESTATEMENT OF TRUSTS ch. 11, introductory note, at 1093 (1935).

[199] RESTATEMENT (SECOND) OF TRUSTS § 348, comment f (1959).

[200] 281 N.Y. 115, 22 N.E.2d 305 (1939), *noted in* 40 COLUM. L. REV. 550 (1940); 53 HARV. L. REV. 327 (1939).

[201] 281 N.Y. at 119-23, 22 N.E.2d at 306-08. *Accord*, RESTATEMENT (SECOND) OF TRUSTS § 348, comment f (1959) (attorney general can enforce restriction); Lefkowitz v. Lebensfeld, 68 A.D.2d 488, 496, 417 N.Y.S.2d 715, 721 (1979), *aff'd*, 51 N.Y.2d 442, 415 N.E.2d 919 (1980) (attorney general can enforce restriction, but where gift is unconditional charitable corporation does not hold property in trust, express or implied).

church corporation as a permanent fund with the income to be used to maintain the church properties did not become available for the general purposes of the Presbytery of Philadelphia, the superior judicatory, when the specific church corporation was dissolved. Instead, the supreme court ruled that under the cy pres power, the presbytery should hold it in trust to apply the income for churches in the county of Philadelphia. The court explained:

The court explained:

> The trust created by the will of testatrix is not a trust in the technical sense of that word as it is used between individuals: Restatement, Trusts, ch. 11, Introductory Note. Where a gift is made directly to a charitable or religious body for purposes which are within the powers of the corporation, it is a trustee for itself, and holds for the purposes specified in the gift. It is, however, a trust in the sense that the fund does not merge into the general property of the corporation but remains under the jurisdiction of a court of equity. Equity has power to define the trust and to restrain any violation of it....
>
> ... [T]his court, with its control and direction of trustees in the use and disposition of property belonging to corporate charities, exercises broad visitorial and supervisory powers of the commonwealth, and its jurisdiction is exclusive.[202]

Consistent with the foregoing reasoning, by the weight of authority, a specific restriction to one of the purposes of a charitable corporation, or a gift to it of a fund specifying that only the income can be used currently, is valid and enforceable by a court of equity just as if the gift were in trust. By the same token, the weight of authority holds that the cy pres power is applicable to a charitable corporation, just as to a charitable trust.[203] On the other hand, the evident differences between trust and corporate ownership are honored in the fact that a corporation is not required to file regular accounting proceedings as if it were a trustee, nor is it subject to normal rules of trust administration, such as the rules against delegation and commingling. Further, a charitable corporation, unlike a trustee, is subject to

---

[202] *In re* Craig's Estate, 356 Pa. 564, 567, 569, 52 A.2d 650, 651-52 (1947).

[203] 4 A. SCOTT, *supra* note 20, § 348.1; G. BOGERT, *supra* note 27, § 431.

direct action by claimants and other creditors.[204] Under Scott's approach, the court should not ask whether the charitable corporation holds its property in a charitable trust, but instead should focus on which one of the incidents of the charitable trust is at issue and then make the decision on principle and authority whether that particular incident should apply to a charitable corporation.

The number of cases cited by both Bogert and Scott as saying that a charitable corporation holds its property in trust is approximately equal to the number they cite as saying that it does not.[205] Few, if any, of these cases offer any assistance in determining the extent of the attorney general's common-law "enforcement" or "supervisory" powers over charitable corporations. Almost all of Bogert's cases involve circumstances in which the court found an express trust for purposes of sustaining the validity of the disposition, enforcing a restriction, or applying the cy pres power. Those three categories predominate in Scott's cases also, with most of the rest being opinions using trust language in resolving some controversy under state tax laws.

Despite a search covering hundreds of trust opinions, including a fifty-state Lexis search covering the principal categories discussed in this section, the author of this Article has not found a single case outside of California in which the "trust" nature of a religious charitable corporation's relationship to its property or its charitable purpose was the basis for any regulatory or supervisory action against the corporation by the attorney general. In short, as to religious charitable corporations the attorney general's so-called common-law powers of enforcement or supervision are nonexistent except for the conventional quo warranto power to limit a corporation to activities

---

[204] *See generally*, Note, *The Charitable Corporation*, 64 HARV. L. REV. 1168 (1951); Comment, *Trusts—Gifts to Charitable Corporations—Nature of Interest Created—Duties of Trustee*, 26 S. CAL. L. REV. 80 (1952).

[205] G. BOGERT, *supra* note 27, § nn.13-14; 4 A. SCOTT, *supra* note 20, § 348.1 nn.4-5. For state-by-state summaries of cases on this subject, see Blackwell, *The Charitable Corporation and the Charitable Trust*, 24 WASH. U.L.Q. 1 (1938); Comment, *A Question on Gifts to Charitable Corporations*, 25 VA. L. REV. 764 (1939).

within its charter powers. This common-law position is in force in all American states except where modified by statute, as discussed in the next Part. As to this subject, the statutes have made few modifications.

IV

State Legislation
for the Supervision
of Charitable Trusts
and Corporations

Because of the absence or ambiguity of adequate common-law powers to enforce and supervise the administration of charitable trusts and corporations, about half of the states have supplemented the attorney general's (and sometimes the equity court's) powers by legislation. The draftsmen of the Uniform Supervision of Trustees for Charitable Purposes Act stated their assumption that most attorneys general "now have the power and duty to compel the proper administration of funds" held for charitable purposes, but argued that new legislation was "vitally needed" because of "the large amount of the national wealth now devoted to charitable purposes, and the complete lack of any practical machinery for supervision by the states."[206] New Hampshire led out in 1943 with the first compre-

---

[206] Uniform Supervision of Trustees for Charitable Purposes Act, Commissioner's Prefatory note, 7A U.L.A. 745, 745-46 (1978) [hereinafter cited as Uniform Act].

hensive legislation, which gave the attorney general investigatory powers and required all public trusts to register and file annual reports.[207] By 1954, four other states, California, Ohio, Rhode Island, and South Carolina, had enacted similar legislation,[208] and in that year the National Association of Attorneys General and the National Conference of Commissioners on Uniform State Laws completed and proposed the Uniform Supervision of Trustees for Charitable Purposes Act.[209]

Support for the Uniform Act was attributed to the fact that the attorney general, in Bogert's words, "has proved a poor guardian of the welfare of charitable gifts." Busy with more pressing duties, he has also been handicapped by "lack of knowledge of the existence of charities within his jurisdiction and of the facts as to performance or breach."[210] Another scholar even urged what he called the "welfare-state argument." Government's large-scale entry into fields formerly left to private charities made it necessary that "charities operat[ing] in the same area as the government . . . should be closely supervised lest they interfere with or duplicate government services."[211] Legislation was also needed to give the attorney general enforcement, in-

---

[207] 1943 N.H. Laws ch. 181. Under this legislation the attorney general had no power to supervise property owned absolutely by a charitable hospital corporation. Portsmouth Hosp. v. Attorney General, 104 N.H. 51, 178 A.2d 516 (1962). Pre-1943 legislation on this subject is discussed in Bogert, *Proposed Legislation Regarding State Supervision of Charities*, 52 MICH. L. REV. 633, 639-41 (1954).

[208] Bogert, *supra* note 207, at 641-49; *see* Corporations Code Act, ch. 1038, 1947 Cal. Stats. 2309; Act of June 30, 1953, 1953 Ohio Laws 351; Act of Apr. 24, 1950, ch. 2617, 1950 R.I. Pub. Laws 739; Act of July 1, 1953, ch. 274, 1953 S.C. Acts 347.

[209] The history of the Uniform Act is reviewed in Bogert, *supra* note 207, at 649-58. *See also* Comment, *Supervision of Charitable Trusts*, 21 U. CHI. L. REV. 118 (1953).

[210] Bogert, *supra* note 207, at 634-35; Comment note 209 *supra*.

[211] Karst, *The Efficiency of the Charitable Dollar: An Unfulfilled State Responsibility*, 73 HARV. L. REV. 433, 479-80 (1960).

vestigative, and supervisory powers that were either nonexistent or subject to serious doubt under the common law.[212]

The Uniform Act directs the attorney general to establish a register of trustees (including corporations) subject to the Act.[213] It also requires trustees to file copies of their governing instruments[214] and (in accordance with rules promulgated by the attorney general) to make regular reports of their assets and administration "which will enable him to ascertain whether they are being properly administered."[215] The attorney general is also authorized to "investigate transactions and relationships of trustees subject to this act for the purpose of determining whether the property held for charitable purposes is properly administered,"[216] to require parties to appear or to produce records,[217] and to institute judicial proceedings "to secure compliance with this act, and to secure the proper administration of any trust or other relationship to which this act applies."[218] The "register, copies of instruments and the reports filed with the Attorney General" are required to be "open to public inspection."[219]

Although the Uniform Act has been formally adopted in only five states,[220] the momentum of the effort to confer legislative powers to

---

[212] Kutner & Koven, *Charitable Trust Legislation in the Several States*, 61 Nw. U.L. REV. 411 (1966); Comment, *The Enforcement of Charitable Trusts*, 18 SYRACUSE L. REV. 618, 625 (1967).

[213] UNIFORM ACT, *supra* note 206, § 4.

[214] *Id.* § 5.

[215] *id.* § 6.

[216] *Id.* § 8.

[217] *Id.*

[218] *Id.* § 11.

[219] *id.* § 10.

[220] CAL. GOV'T CODE §§ 12580-12597 (West 1980); Charitable Trust Act §§ 1-14 ILL. REV. SSTAT. ch 14, §§ 51-64 (1963); MICH. COMP. LAWS ANN. §§ 14.251-.266 (1967); MINN. STAT. ANN. §§ 501.71-.81 (West Supp. 1981); OR. REV. STAT. §§ 128.610-.750 (1980).

supervise charitable activities[221] and the thoughtful example of the uniform legislation have contributed to the enactment of other comprehensive legislation in a total of ten additional states.[222] In addition, ten other states have some statutory provisions authorizing the attorney general to enforce charitable trusts.[223]

One of the most contested points in the debate over the Uniform Act was whether (or the extent to which) it should apply to charitable corporations. The final version excludes from its coverage "a charitable corporation organized and operated primarily for educational, religious, or hospital purposes."[224] Following distinctions already established in the case law, the Uniform Act does provide for supervisory authority over "any corporation which has accepted property to be used for a particular charitable corporate purpose as distinguished from the general purposes of the corporation formed for the

---

[221] *E.g.*, Karst, note 211 *supra*; Howland, *The History of the Supervision of Charitable Trusts and Corporations in California*, 13 U.C.L.A. L. REV. 1029 (1966); E. FISCH, D. FREED, & E. SCHACHTER, *supra* note 19, § 683; M. FREMONT-SMITH, FOUNDATIONS AND GOVERNMENT (1965).

[222] HAWAII REV. STAT. §§ 467B-1 TO -12 (1980); MD. ANN. CODE art. 41, §§ 103A-103L (1980); MD. EST. & TRUSTS CODE ANN. §§ 14-301 to -308 (1974); MASS. GEN. LAWS ANN. ch. 12 §§ 8-8K (West 1976); N.H. REV. STAT. ANN. §§ 7:19 to :32-a (1970); N.Y. EST., POWERS, & TRUSTS LAW §§ 8-1.1 to .7 (McKinney 1967); N.C. GEN. STAT. §§ 36A-47 to -54 (Supp. 1979); OHIO REV. CODE ANN. §§ 109.23-.33 (Page 1978); R.I. GEN. LAWS §§ 18-9-1 to -16 (1969); S.C. CODE §§ 21-31-10 to -40 (1976); WASH. REV. CODE ANN. §§ 19.10.010-.900 (1978). *See generally* G. BOGERT, *supra* note 27, § 411, at 420-24; Kutner & Koven, note 212 *supra*. The statutes are analyzed in E. FISCH, D. FREED & E. SCHACHTER, *supra* note 19, §§ 679-695.

[223] CONN. GEN. STAT. ANN. § 3-125 (West 1969); GA. CODE ANN. § 108-212 (1979); IDAHO CODE § 67-1401 (1980); ME. REV. STAT. ANN. tit. 5, § 194 (1979); NEB. REV. STAT. § 21-614 (1977); NEV. REV. STAT. § 165.230 (1979); N.D. CENT. CODE ANN. § 59-04-02 (1960); S.D. COMP. LAWS ANN. § 55-9-5 (1980); TENN. CODE ANN. § 23-2802 (1956); WIS. STAT. ANN. § 701.10(3) (West 1981).

[224] UNIFORM ACT, *supra* note 206, § 3. This section also excludes "an officer of a religious organization who holds property for religious purposes."

administration of a charitable trust."[225] However, in adopting the Uniform Act, and in enacting other comprehensive legislation, most states extended the scope of their legislation beyond those limited categories to include some types of charitable corporations.[226]

The one type of charity that is universally excluded or omitted from the coverage of charitable enforcement or supervision legislation is the church or the trust, corporation, or other organization formed for religious purposes. All fifteen of the states that have enacted the Uniform Act or other comprehensive supervisory legislation expressly exclude religious corporations, trusts, or other religious organizations from their coverage.[227] These exclusions

---

[225] *Id.* § 2.

[226] Cal. Gov't Code § 12581 (West 1980); Hawaii Rev. Stat. § 467B-2 (1976); Charitable Trust Act, Ill. Rev. Stat. ch. 14 § 53 (1963); Md. Ann. Code art. 41 § 103A (1978); Mass. Gen. Laws Ann. ch. 12, § 8 (West 1976); Mich. Comp. Laws Ann. § 14.251 (1967); Minn. Stat. Ann. § 501.71 (West Supp. 1981); N.H. Rev. Stat. Ann. § 7:19 (1970); N.Y. Est., Powers, & Trusts Law § 8-1.4 (McKinney 1967); N.C. Gen. Stat. § 36A-47 (Supp. 1979); Ohio Rev. Code Ann. § 109.23 (Page 1978); Or. Rev. Stat. § 128.620 (1980); R.I. Gen. Laws § 18-9-4 (1969); Wash. Rev. Code Ann. § 19.10.020 (1978).

[227] Cal. Gov't Code § 12583 (West 1980); Hawaii Rev. Stat. § 467B-11)(1976); Charitable Trust Act, Ill. Rev. Stat. ch. 14 § 54 (1963); Md. Ann. Code art. 41, § 103C (1978); Mass. Gen. Laws Ann. ch. 12 § 8F (West 1976); Mich. Comp. Laws Ann. § 14.253 (1967); Minn. Stat. Ann. § 501.74 (West Supp. 1981); N.H. Rev. Stat. Ann. § 7:19 (1970); N.Y. Est., Powers, & Trust Law § 8-1.4(b) (McKinney 1967); N.C. Gen. Stat. § 36A-47 (Supp. 1979); Or. Rev. Stat. § 128.640 (1980); R.I. Gen. Law § 18-9-15 (1969); S.C. Code § 21-31-50 (1976); Wash. Rev. Code Ann. § 19.10.020 (1978). In Ohio, the attorney general is empowered to make exemptions by regulation, and has exempted religious organizations. Ohio Rev. Code Ann. § 109.26 (Page 1978); Ohio Adm. Code § 109:1-1-02(B)(3) (1980). These exemption provisions cover all of the comprehensive enactments cited in notes 220 and 222 *supra*. The more restrictive enforcement authorizations cited in note 223 *supra* are typically so general that it is uncertain whether they apply to religious corporations or trusts in the first place. On a related subject, the various state statutes authorizing incorporation by religious bodies are cited and analyzed in Kauper & Ellis, *supra* note 94, at 1527-57.

were apparently intended to avoid questions about the constitutionality of supervisory legislation and strong political opposition to its passage.[228]

This review of modern legislation for the supervision of charitable trusts and corporations shows the following: (1) Concern over the inadequacy or ambiguity of the attorney general's common-law powers to enforce and supervise charities and the total lack of practical machinery for the official supervision of wealth devoted to charitable purposes have stimulated the enactment of comprehensive legislation in fifteen states and individual enforcement provisions in ten others; (2) most of the comprehensive legislation empowers the attorney general to exercise some supervisory authority over charitable corporations as well as charitable trusts; (3) but without exception, this comprehensive supervisory legislation provides that charitable corporations or trusts for religious purposes will not be subject to the registration, reporting, enforcement, or other supervisory powers of the attorney general.

Therefore, in virtually every state, the attorney general has no statutory powers to enforce or supervise religious charitable trusts or corporations. In this area he must rely on his common-law powers. As discussed earlier, those powers are limited as to charitable trusts,[229] even more limited as to charitable corporations,[230] and virtually nonexistent as to churches and other corporations and trusts for religious purposes.[231] This statement is true in every state but California, whose unique history will be discussed in the next Part.

---

[228] E. FISCH, D. FREED & E. SCHACHTER, *supra* note 19, § 685; Bogert, *supra* note 207, at 646 (comment on Ohio exemption).

[229] *See* text accompanying notes 126-60 *supra.*

[230] *See* text accompanying notes 161-90 *supra.*

[231] *See* text accompanying notes 178-90 *supra.*

V

CALIFORNIA CASES
AND STATUTES

In California, decisions on church property disputes and on attorney general and judicial supervision of charitable trusts and corporations (including religious organizations) have contributed to a common stream that has eroded traditional barriers separating church and state in other jurisdictions. In California, the discredited implied trust doctrine, which originally evolved as a means of settling church property disputes, came to be used as authority for a series of common-law decisions and statutory enactments that gave a broad supervisory jurisdiction to the attorney general. That supervisory authority was, in turn, the apparent stimulus for the attorney general to take a more active role in the settlement of church property disputes and in the dissolution of churches than that officer has taken in other jurisdictions. The history of the unique California common and statutory law leading to the so-called "public trust doctrine," which is still the subject of active consideration by the California Legislature, is therefore worthy of special attention.

California's use of trust doctrines to resolve church property controversies began in 1889 in *Baker v. Ducker*.[232] This was a contest over which schismatic group should succeed to property purchased with funds church members had contributed "for the erection of a parsonage for the First Reformed Congregation of Stockton."[233] The church's articles of incorporation showed that its purpose was "to provide its members with the preaching of the Gospel, the administration of the sacraments, and the other means of grace in accordance with the confessions of faith known as the Heidelberg Catechism," and that the church was to be subject to the discipline of the Reformed Church of the United States, a national hierarchical religious society.[234] After a time, a majority of the congregation came to prefer Lutheran doctrine. The congregation then engaged a minister of that faith, and their elected trustees changed the name of the corporation to the First German Evangelical Lutheran Zion Society of Stockton and declared that they had no connection with any superior ecclesiastical body. In a contest over ownership of the parsonage the adherents to the original Heidelberg doctrine argued the implied trust theory; the majority, who preferred the Lutheran doctrine, cited cases rejecting the implied trust and holding that those who governed the corporation (in this case, a majority of the congregation) could direct the disposition of its property.[235] Relying on a handful of cases, including the Pennsylvania decision in *Schnorr's Appeal*,[236] the California Supreme Court adopted the implied trust theory:

> It is thus made clear that the property in question was held by the Reformed Church in trust for its members, and the defendants, even

---

[232] 79 Cal. 365 (1889).

[233] *Id.* at 373.

[234] *Id.*

[235] *E.g.*, Robertson v. Bullions, 11 N.Y. 243 (1854), discussed in text accompanying note 93 *supra*.

[236] 67 Pa. 138 (1870), discussed in text accompanying note 108 *supra*.

though they constituted a majority of the members, had no right and no power to divert it to the use of another and different church organization.[237]

The implied trust doctrine was reaffirmed, expanded, and lodged solidly in California law in *Wheelock v. First Presbyterian Church*,[238] decided in 1897. In *Wheelock* a Presbyterian congregation had divided over where its new church should be constructed. When the corporation's trustees followed the wishes of the majority, purchasing land and proceeding with construction, the minority appealed to the supervisory church tribunal. The presbytery divided the congregation into two organizations and apportioned its funds in proportion to membership, 53 percent and 47 percent. When the majority faction, which controlled the corporation, refused to pay the minority its share, the supreme court used an implied trust theory to compel payment.[239] The court said that the corporation was "a trustee holding property for the use and enjoyment of the church, and every member of the church is a beneficiary of that trust."[240] True to the doctrine of their church and faithful to the decree of their ruling ecclesiastical authority, the minority's plaintiff's were "beneficiaries of the trust before the presbytery divided the church, and, in justice and equity, must stand in the same position after division." A court of equity would therefore "deem it for the best interests of all

---

[237] 79 Cal. at 374 *Cf.* Horsman v. Allen, 129 Cal. 131, 61 P. 796 (1900) (alteration of church constitution by two-thirds membership upheld when change didn't destroy church's identity).

[238] 119 Cal. 477, 51 P. 841 (1897).

[239] The trial court had denied relief on the basis that a pro rata division of property was not appropriate in the case of an incorporated body when there had been no statutory dissolution proceedings. Baker v. Ducker, 79 Cal. 365 (1889), was apparently thought inapplicable on the ground that the implied trust only ensured that church property would continue dedicated to a particular religious doctrine. In contrast, this was a case in which the congregation had divided over an administrative controversy (location of church) rather than a doctrinal one.

[240] 119 Cal. at 483, 51 P. at 844. The court cites Weinbrenner v. Colder, 43 Pa. 244, 249 (1844), but the quoted language does not appear in that source.

concerned that the trust fund be . . . apportioned according to the numerical strength of each."[241] As in *Baker v. Ducker*, the court specifically rejected decisions from New York and other jurisdictions that resolved such controversies by deferring to the majority or other governing body of the church corporation.[242] The attorney general was not a party to either of these cases.

The role and authority of the attorney general was at issue in *People v. Cogswell*,[243] which involved a suit against a donor to establish the validity of a charitable trust to create a polytechnic college. In ruling that the attorney general had standing to bring this suit, the supreme court said:

> This action is based upon averments of a public trust. It is brought to remedy abuses in the management of this trust. It is not only the right, but the duty of the attorney general to prosecute such an action. The state, as parens patriae, superintends the management of all public charities or trusts, and in these matters acts through her attorney general.[244]

The court's comments as to remedying "abuses in the management" were dicta since allegations on that subject had been settled by stipulation. The only issue on appeal was the validity of the trust, which the attorney general clearly had common-law authority to establish and defend against the donor's attempts to regain the property.[245] Nevertheless, the above passage is frequently cited as a leading statement of the California attorney general's common-law authority to "remedy abuses" and to "superintend the management" of a chari-

---

[241] 119 Cal. at 484, 51 P. at 844.

[242] The basis of distinction, that religious and other charitable corporations could not hold their property in trust in New York because charitable trusts were invalid in this state (*Id.* at 486, 51 P. at 845) was erroneous, since New York's rejection of the implied trust theory for charitable corporations predated the invalidity of charitable corporations in that state. *See* note 190 *supra*.

[243] 113 Cal. 129, 45 P. 270 (1896).

[244] *Id.* at 136, 45 P. at 271.

[245] *See* text accompanying note 34 *supra*.

table trust.[246] The court's declaration, of course, goes well beyond the common-law powers recognized in either England or the other American states.

In *In re McDole's Estate*,[247] decided in 1932, the California Supreme Court made its first reference to the implied trust theory in a case involving charitable trust validity and administration rather than a church property dispute.[248] The problem arose when a testator bequeathed the residue of his estate to "the Stubblefield Home for the Aged," which was not incorporated or otherwise capable of taking the title to property. The heirs urged that the disposition was invalid, but the court disagreed. The testator had used the name of a home operated by three trustees under an earlier testamentary trust, and the court held that the gift was, in effect, a gift to the trustees upon an implied trust whose terms, clearly reminiscent of the trust used to resolve church property controversies, were sufficiently precise to avoid the fatal indefiniteness:

> A devise to society or corporation organized for a charitable purpose without further declaration of the use to which the gift is to be put, is given in trust to carry out the objects for which the organization was

---

[246] *E.g, In re* Los Angeles County Pioneer Soc'y, 246 P.2d 1029, 1033 (1952), *aff'd*, 40 Cal. 2d 852, 257 P.2d 1 (1953); Brown v. Memorial Nat'l Home Foundation, 162 Cal. App. 2d 513, 536-37, 329 P.2d 118 (1958) (construing CAL. CORP. CODE § 9505 (West 1977) (repealed in 1980).

[247] 215 Cal. 328, 10 P.2d 75 (1932).

[248] Omitted from text discussion is a succession of intervening California decisions on the application of charitable trust theory under section 1313 of the Civil Code, a mortmain provision placing a one-third maximum on the proportion of an estate that a testator can leave to a charitable corporation or in trust for a charitable use within a specified period before death. *In re* Hamilton's Estate, 181 Cal. 758, 186 P. 587 (1919) (trust to say masses is charitable); *In re* Dol's Estate, 182 Cal. 159, 187 P. 428 (1920) (absolute gift to incorporated mutual benefit hospital not a gift in trust to a charitable donee); *In re* Lubin's Estate, 186 Cal. 326, 199 P. 15 (1921) (bequest to incorporated Jewish congregation was charitable gift); *In re* Fitzgerald's Estate, 62 Cal. App. 744, 750, 217 P. 773, 775-76 (1923) (absolute bequest to Catholic Bishop, a corporation sole, was charitable gift for purposes of § 1313 since it could only be used for the charter purposes of the corporation, which were charitable).

created.... [249] Similarly a devise to trustees who maintain a home for orphan children and indigent widows is upon trust to apply the property for the maintenance and care of those persons who reside in the home.[250]

As to corporations, the first sentence was dictum, since this case did not involve a corporate donee. Nevertheless, this case has frequently been cited as an expression of a California common-law rule that charitable corporations hold their unrestricted donations on an implied trust for their corporate purposes (rather than subject to the internal governance involved in the principle of corporate autonomy recognized elsewhere). This "common-law rule" has also been codified in the California legislation mentioned below.

In 1947 the California Legislature reaffirmed and updated its Nonprofit Corporations Law[251] and also enacted comprehensive

---

[249] Here the court cited one treatise and three cases. The citation to "2 Perry on Trusts (7th Ed.) p. 1258" is a reference to the implied trust doctrine in church property disputes. *In re* Winchester's Estate, 133 Cal. 271, 65 P. 475 (1901), the only California case, upheld a bequest to an unincorporated natural history society because the use was clearly charitable and equity would not allow the trust to fail for want of a trustee. The other two cited cases do not support the court's proposition either: Dickenson v. City of Anna, 310 Ill. 222, 141 N.E. 754 (1923) (gift to charitable corporation was charitable for purposes of rule against perpetuities; no reference to corporate donee's holding "in trust"); Rhode Island Hosp. Trust Co. v. Williams, 50 R.I. 385, 148 A. 189 (1929) (cy pres applied to unrestricted gift to charitable corporation; no reference to corporate donee's holding "in trust").

[250] 215 Cal. at 334, 10 P.2d at 77, (citations omitted), *followed in In re* DeMars' Estate, 20 Cal. App. 2d 514, 67 P.2d 374 (1937) (devise to unincorporated hospital held valid charitable trust; court appointed trustee); Estate of Clippinger, 75 Cal. App. 2d 426, 171 P.2d 567 (1946) (gift to trustee of unincorporated association held valid charitable gift).

[251] In 1931, in the predecessor to CAL. CORP. CODE § 9505 (West 1977) (repealed in 1980), the legislature had provided that a nonprofit corporation

> which holds property subject to any public or charitable trust shall be subject at all times to examination [by the attorney general] to ascertain the conditions of its affairs and to what extent, if at all, it

code provisions governing the new category of "Corporations for Charitable Purposes."[252] The attorney general's powers as to charitable corporations were essentially identical to the code powers he had enjoyed over nonprofit corporations since 1931—"to ascertain the condition of its affairs and to what extent, if at all, it may fail to comply with trusts which it has assumed or may depart from the general purpose for which it is formed," with authority to institute "the proceedings necessary to correct the noncompliance or departure" (section 10207).[253] But, unlike the earlier Nonprofit Corporations Law, the new code provisions on charitable corporations had a specific section on the corporation's relationship to contributed assets. A charitable corporation could hold assets on an express trust, or it could take property and funds "without specification of any charitable or eleemosynary purpose." In the latter case, "the property or funds so received shall, nevertheless, be held upon the trust that they shall be used for charitable and eleemosynary purposes" (section 10206(c)).[254] By this enactment California seems to have codified the doctrine of implied trust as to unrestricted donations to charitable corporations.

The California Supreme Court applied the new code provisions for the first time in its 1953 decision, *In re Los Angeles County Pioneer*

---

may fail to comply with trusts which it has assumed or may depart from the general purposes for which it is formed.

Act of June 12, 1931, ch. 871, § 605(c), 1931 Cal. Stat. 1847, 1852. In case of any such failure or departure, the attorney general was authorized to institute "the proceedings necessary to correct the same." *Id.* While referring specifically to express trusts ("trusts which it has assumed"), this 1931 statute was, of course, neutral on the question whether a charitable corporation held its absolute gifts in trust for its corporate purposes.

[252] Corporations Code Act, ch. 1038, §§ 10200-10208, 1947 Cal. Stat. 2309, 2419-22.

[253] *Id.* § 10207, 1947 Cal. Stat. 2309, 2421-22 (codified as CAL. CORP. CODE § 10207 (West 1977) (repealed 1980).

[254] *Id.* § 10206(c), 1947 Cal. Stat. 2309, 2421 (codified as CAL. CORP. CODE § 10206(c) (West 1977) (repealed 1980). For an excellent summary of the law just a few years after this statute, see Note, 26 S. CAL. L. REV. 80 (1952).

Society.[255] *Los Angeles Pioneer Society* involved an attempt to dissolve a corporation devoted to commemorating historical events and to distribute its assets among its members. Citing common-law authorities, the supreme court decided that the attorney general could intervene since he was " a necessary party to proceedings affecting the disposition of assets of a charitable trust."[256] The court relied on code section 10207 as the sole authority for its ruling that "when assets are held by a charitable corporation, as here, the duty to protect such assets is expressly placed upon the Attorney General by the Corporations Code."[257] The court concluded this point as follows:

> Under the Corporations Code a charitable corporation is subject to the same supervision by the Attorney General as is a non-profit corporation holding its assets subject to a charitable trust, §§ 9505, 10207; see, 26 So. Cal. L. Rev. 80, and deviations from the purposes stated in Pioneer's articles are thus subject to the same corrective measures that would be taken against a trustee of a charitable trust that similarly refused to carry out its duties.[258]

The supreme court affirmed the trial court's judgment, appointing a successor trustee to continue the commemorative activities.

In *Los Angeles Pioneer Society*, the California attorney general, who had not even been a party to the church property disputes and the charitable trust administration cases discussed thus far, became the central figure in the enforcement and supervision of an implied trust in the case of charitable corporations. The attorney general's supervisory jurisdiction was thereby enlarged to reach property held by charitable corporations that was beyond his reach under the common-law in other states (except as to express trusts) and even by the common law of California, except for the dictum in *In re McDole's Estate.*[259]

---

[255] 40 Cal. 2d 852, 257 P.2d 1 (1953).

[256] *Id.* at 861, 257 P.2d at 6.

[257] *Id.*

[258] *Id.*

[259] *Pioneer* cited the *McDole* case approvingly, along with an appellate opinion that relied on it. *Id.* at 860, 257 P.2d at 6.

The attorney general's supervisory powers over *religious* charitable corporations or trusts remained doubtful. The religious institution was not mentioned specifically in the legislation on charitable corporations, and up to this point had not been involved in any supervision case decided by the California courts. Although not on center stage, a church was waiting in the wings in the supreme court's decision in *Pacific Home v. Los Angeles County.*[260] In *Pacific Home* the issue was whether the taxpayer corporation's old-age home for Methodist leaders qualified for tax exemption. The state opposed exemption because upon dissolution the taxpayer's assets would go to the local conference of the Methodist Church, whose corporate articles would permit them to be used for nonexempt social as well as religious and charitable purposes. The court rejected this argument and ruled for the taxpayer because the corporation's properties were deemed to be impresssed with a charitable trust "for the declared corporate purposes," which the attorney general had duty to enforce. It followed, the court said, "that neither plaintiff nor its successor could legally divert its assets to any purpose other than charitable purposes, and said property was therefore 'irrevocably dedicated' to exempt purposes."[261]

This was the first case suggesting that the attorney general could enforce a trust against a church corporation, the Methodist Conference. In the peculiar hypothetical circumstances discussed in this tax case, however, it appears that if the Methodist Conference took the property as successor of Pacific Homes it would be, in effect, the trustee of an *express* trust, so the court's and the attorney general's enforcement role would be no more than an exercise of their familiar powers to enforce (establish the validity of) an express charitable trust against any person or corporation who was the trustee.

In 1959, California became the first state to enact the Uniform Supervision of Trustees for Charitable Purposes Act.[262] This statute

---

[260] 41 Cal. 2d 844, 264 P.2d 539 (1953).

[261] *Id.* at 852, 264 P.2d at 542-43.

[262] Act of June 30, 1959, ch. 1258, 1959 Cal. Stats. 3396 (codified as CAL. GOV'T CODE §§ 12580-12597 (West 1980). *See generally* Howland, note 221 *supra*.

underlined the existing ambiguity concerning the attorney general's supervisory authority over religious charitable trusts or corporations in California, since it stated that it did not apply "to any religious corporation sole or other religious corporation or organization which holds property for religious purposes."[263] Subject to that exception, as noted earlier, the uniform legislation gave the attorney general clear statutory authority to exercise registration, reporting, and enforcement powers over charitable trusts.[264]

In contrast to his inactivity with respect to religious charitable trusts and corporations, the California attorney general was very active in the 1950s, 1960s, and 1970s in enforcement measures designed to ensure that the assets of other charitable institutions continued to be committed to their charitable purpose. To mention only cases that reached the appellate level, in 1958 the attorney general obtained declaratory relief to resolve conflicting claims to the assets of charitable trusts created for Gold Star mothers.[265] Later he sued a nonprofit corporation and its distributees in dissolution to impress a charitable trust upon property that the corporation had allegedly held in trust.[266] When charitable corporations refused to accept property devised to them or were unable to accept it because they were no longer viable, the attorney general obtained the ap-

---

[263] CAL. GOV'T CODE § 12583 (West 1980).

[264] See discussion in text accompanying notes 212-19 supra; 7 B. WITKIN, SUMMARY OF CALIFORNIA LAW § 37 (8th ed. 1974).

[265] Brown v. Memorial Nat'l Home Foundation, 162 Cal. App. 2d 513, 329 P.2d 118 (1958). In contrast, the attorney general had not even been a party in two cases that came to the supreme court six years earlier involving property disputes between different factions in a *church*. Providence Baptist Church v. Superior Court, 40 Cal. 2d 55, 251 P.2d 10 (1952); Rosicrucian Fellowship v. Rosicrucian Fellowship Nonsectarian Church, 39 Cal. 2d 121, 245 P.2d 481 (1952).

[266] Lynch v. Spilman, 67 Cal. 2d 251, 261, 431 P.2d 636, 642, 62 Cal. Rptr. 12, 18 (1967) (held: trust could be imposed if property originally held for charitable purposes, a matter to be determined at trial). *See also* Veterans' Indus., Inc. v. Lynch, 8 Cal. App. 3d 902, 88 Cal. Rptr. 303 (1970) (cy pres to name successor on dissolution).

pointment of alternate trustees under the doctrine of cy pres.[267] The attorney general was held to be an indispensable party in a proceeding to fill vacancies among the cotrustees of a charitable trust,[268] and he had standing to object to an order settling claims to accumulated income in a charitable remainder trust.[269] Finally, in a case decided in 1970, the attorney general invoked his statutory supervisory authority over charitable corporations[270] to obtain a judgment surcharging corporate officers and replacing them for mismanagement in failing to invest charitable funds and make them productive.[271] None of these cases involved churches or religious uses.

The first California case using the implied trust doctrine to support supervisory jurisdiction over church corporations was the court of appeal decision in *Metropolitan Baptist Church of Richmond, Inc. v. Younger.*[272] The church in *Metropolitan Baptist* was incorporated in

---

[267] *In re* Estate of Faulkner, 128 Cal. App. 2d 575, 275 P.2d 818 (1954) (corporation refused to accept gift); *In re* Estate of Connolly, 48 Cal. App. 3d 129, 121 Cal. Rptr. 325 (1975) (corporation no longer viable). For another cy pres case, see note 266 *supra.*

[268] *In re* Estate of Schloss, 56 Cal. 2d 248, 363 P.2d 875, 14 Cal. Rptr. 643 (1961))(petition by cotrustee—attorney general not a party).

[269] *In re* Estate of Horton, 11 Cal. App. 3d 680, 90 Cal. Rptr. 66 (1970). Although the court said that the attorney general was "an overseer of charities representing the public," with standing to seek redress in the courts for contracts entered into by charities which are collusive or tainted by fraud or which demonstrate any abuse of trust management, the court held that it had been cited to no "authority placing the Attorney General in the position of a super administrator of charities" with authority to participate in or veto its contractual undertakings. *Id.* at 685-86, 90 Cal. Rptr. at 68-69. The trustee's settlement was approved despite the attorney general's objection.

[270] CAL. CORP. CODE § 1027 (West 1977) (repealed 1980).

[271] Lynch v. John M. Redfield Foundation, 9 Cal. App. 3d 293, 88 Cal. Rptr. 86 (1970).

[272] 48 Cal. App. 3d 850, 121 Cal. Rptr. 899 (1975). A Church was involved in People v. Christ's Church of the Golden Rule, 79 Cal. App. 2d 858, 181 P.2d 49 (1947), but in that case the appeal was dismissed for lack of an appealable order. There the attorney general had sought the removal of the trustee of Christ's Church of the Golden Rule, an accounting of the corpo-

1956 as a California nonprofit corporation. Its articles of incorporation and uncontradicted extrinsic evidence showed that the purpose of its founders was to establish "a Baptist church in Richmond, Contra Costa County, to preach and teach the Scriptures in that city in essential accord with the beliefs of fundamental Baptist churches."[273] When the church's membership fell to six, including the pastor and his family, the congregation voted unanimously to dissolve the corporation and to distribute its $25,000 net assets (proceeds of member contributions) in specified fractions to fundamental Baptist churches in Dublin and Oakland, California, and Harlan, Iowa, and to a nondenominational seminary and a servicemen's center, also in California. The church petitioned the court for authority to distribute its assets in accordance with the membership decision, making the attorney general a party as required by statute. Both the attorney general and the trial court opposed the church's plan of distribution. The attorney general proposed that the assets be held in trust for the benefit of another fundamental Baptist church in Contra Costa County, if one should be formed. In a decree that was affirmed by the court of appeal, the trial court rejected that proposal as "not viable" and also rejected the church's plan because some of its proposed distributes were not churches and the Iowa congregation was too distant.[274] Ruling that the church held its property in trust "to carry out the objects for which the organization was created,"[275] objects that had now become impossible, the trial and

---

ration's assets, and the appointment of a receiver pending the accounting. His complaint alleged that the church, a nonprofit California corporation with assets exceeding $3 million, was completely dominated by the trustee, who had been guilty of unauthorized expenditures and was about to sell corporate property and convert the proceeds to his own use. Proceeding ex parte, the trial court removed the trustee and appointed a receiver. Appellant attacked this action as a denial of due process, which left the court without jurisdiction. Inexplicably, there was no argument that the action denied religious freedom.

[273] 48 Cal. App. 3d at 855, 121 Cal. Rptr. at 902.

[274] Id.

[275] Id. at 858, 121 Cal. Rptr. at 903 (quoting Estate of Clippinger, 75 Cal. App. 426, 433, 171 P.2d 567, 572 (1946).

appellate courts applied the cy pres doctrine and modified the "trust" to decree that the church property should be divided equally between the closest fundamental Baptist churches, the ones in Dublin and Oakland, California.

No previous California appellate decision had discussed the constitutionality of the implied trust doctrine under the First Amendment, so the court's treatment of this subject broke new ground in California law. The ruling principle, the court held, was the implied trust doctrine, which embodied what the court referred to as California's "strong public policy that trust property of a nonprofit religious or charitable corporation be not diverted from its declared purpose."[276] Acknowledging that this principle applied to charities in general, the church nevertheless argued that the rule must yield to the First Amendment when a church was involved. Specifically, an autonomous congregation must be allowed to make a binding decision on who should receive its assets in dissolution. Not so, the court held. The First Amendment merely required that the court adjudicate property rights "without resolving underlying controversies over religious doctrine."[277] This was done by applying "neutral principles of law, developed for use in all property disputes," which were "applicable alike to all churches and other charitable organizations."[278] In this case "neutral principles" meant the implied trust doctrine, which safeguarded the property "in accordance with the purpose of the organization's founder and its property's donors," as modified by the court in the exercise of its cy pres powers. Any ecclesiastical concern with this kind of disposition was, the court said, "incidental and remote."[279]

Metropolitan Baptist represents an entirely new application of the implied trust doctrine, even in the case of churches. The case did not

---

[276] 48 Cal. App. 3d at 858, 121 Cal. Rptr. at 903.

[277] *Id.* at 859, 121 Cal. Rptr. at 904 (quoting Presbyterian Church v. Mary E.B. Hull Memorial Presbyterian Church, 393 U.S. 440, 449 (1969), discussed in text accompanying note 355 *infra*.

[278] 48 Cal. App. 3d at 859, 121 Cal. Rptr. at 904.

[279] *Id.*

involve a doctrinal or administrative controversy, resolved by the application of an implied trust to ensure that property continued to be used for the benefit of those who adhered to the original purpose, as did *Baker v. Ducker* or *Wheelock v. First Presbyterian*.[280] In *Metropolitan Baptist* a unanimous church membership resolved how the church's property should be distributed—to designated Baptist churches and to other organizations engaged in religious missions—but the court used the implied trust doctrine to substitute its own plan of distribution. If this represented the application of a "neutral principle," it was no more "neutral" than the rule advocated by the church—that the court give effect to the unanimous decision of the congregation (so long as that decision did not divert the property from an acknowledged charitable purpose). The church's proposal would minimize official intervention in church affairs, whereas the implied trust doctrine advocated by the attorney general and the court inevitably involved those officers in reviewing ecclesiastical decisions and church doctrines and purposes.[281]

Since *Metropolitan Baptist* there have been six California Court of Appeal decisions discussing the application of the implied trust doctrine to churches or religious charitable corporations. The California Supreme Court has never ruled on this question, either from the standpoint of substantive trust law or First Amendment considerations.

The first of the appellate decisions, *Queen of Angels Hospital v. Younger*,[282] prevented a church-related hospital from abandoning its hospital activity and using its property to provide service through clinics. In answer to the church's argument that freedom of religion precluded the kind of scrutiny of religious activities involved in the California statutes and cases unless there was a compelling state in-

---

[280] *See* text accompanying notes 232 & 238 *supra*.

[281] For example, the court designated the two recipients because they were "fundamental Baptist churches," a judgment the court could hardly have made without including some potential recipients and excluding others on the basis of doctrinal considerations about which were "fundamental Baptist" and which were not.

[282] 66 Cal. App. 3d 359, 136 Cal. Rptr. 36 (1977).

terest, the court cited *Metropolitan Baptist* for "the established rule that the application of neutral principles to situations not involving the internal operations of a religious group infringes on no First Amendment rights."[283] This adds little to the earlier ruling.

In contrast, *Wilson v. Hinkle*,[284] a church property dispute, questioned the continued authority of *Metropolitan Baptist*, suggesting that the neutral-principles doctrine recently established by the United States Supreme Court had rendered obsolete that case's reliance on the implied trust doctrine.[285] The implied trust theory was also rejected as a viable means of resolving church property disputes under neutral principles in the *Samoan Congregational* case, discussed below, and in the succeeding cases of *Presbytery of Riverside v. Community Church*,[286] and *Protestant Episcopal Church v. Barker*.[287] As the court observed in *Barker*, "[t]he implied trust theory almost inevitably puts the civil courts squarely in the midst of ecclesiastical controversies."[288]

California's substantial innovations in the application of the implied trust doctrine to churches are best illustrated on the facts of the remaining two cases, *Samoan Congregational*, a church property dis-

---

[283] *Id.* at 370, 136 Cal. Rptr. at 42. The court also said that it was "well-established that a religious group may not claim the protection of the First Amendment with respect to its purely secular activities." *Id.* The "purely secular activities," which the court said did not involve "the internal operations of a religious group," *id.*, included the following from the articles of incorporation quoted by the court: " 'To establish, . . . and operate a hospital . . .; [t]o perform and to foster and support acts of Chrisitan charity . . . to practice, foster and encourage religious beliefs and activities, particularly those of the Holy Roman Catholic Church. . . . ' " *Id.* at 366, 136 Cal. Rptr. at 40.

[284] 67 Cal. App. 3d 506, 136 Cal. Rptr. 731 (1977).

[285] *Id.* at 511-12, 136 Cal. Rptr. at 734-35. The neutral-principles doctrine is discussed in text accompanying notes 355-64 *infra*.

[286] 89 Cal. App. 3d 910, 152 Cal. Rptr. 854 (1979).

[287] 115 Cal. App. 3d 599, 171 Cal. Rptr. 541 (1981).

[288] *Id.* at 618, 171 Cal. Rptr. at 551.

pute, and *Faith Center*, an attorney general supervision case. Both were discussed at the beginning of this Article.

Like the other three cases mentioned above, the *Samoan Congregational*[289] case rejected the use of the implied trust doctrine that California has followed in the resolution of church property controversies for almost a century, since *Baker v. Ducker* and *Wheelock v. First Presbyterian*. The court rebuffed the contention that the church corporation held its assets in trust for the hierarchical association. Instead, the court applied "neutral principles" to look at the corporate articles and bylaws and concluded that they vested control of the corporation and its property in the board of directors and that "there is no intent whatsoever to create either an express or implied trust on behalf of plaintiff or those members who are loyal to the parent church."[290] The implied trust doctrine was rejected on the constitutionally sound basis that a reference to neutral corporate documents and a granting of considerable autonomy to a church corporation will minimize the court's involvement with the doctrinal and ecclesiastical matters necessarily involved in any ascertainment and enforcement of the original purpose of the church corporation's founders or donors.

Where did this approach lead in the resolution of this church property dispute? In the companion *Samoan Congregational* case,[291] which arose on the minority's petition for involuntary dissolution, the court had to decide what to do with the corporation's property. Although neutral as between the contestants, the attorney general insisted that the church assets were impressed with a charitable trust and that therefore they "must be distributed for church purposes under the *cy-pres* doctrine."[292] The contestants agreed and stipulated

---

[289] Samoan Congregational Christian Church in the United States v. Samoan Congregational Christian Church of Oceanside, 66 Cal. App. 3d 69, 135 Cal. Rptr. 793 (1977), discussed in text accompanying note 4 *supra*.

[290] 66 Cal. App. 3d at 78, 135 Cal. Rptr. at 798.

[291] Fuimaono v. Samoan Congregational Christian Church of Oceanside, 66 Cal. App. 3d 80, 135 Cal. Rptr. 799 (1977).

[292] *Id.* at 83, 135 Cal. Rptr. at 800.

that if the court found for the plaintiff, the assets should be transferred to another corporation serving the same area. This was apparently the order entered by the trial court, which was affirmed on appeal. In view of the court's apparent rejection of the implied trust doctrine and its heavy reliance on corporate autonomy, who would have received the property on dissolution if there had been no stipulation? Under the implied trust theory, the court in *Metropolitan Baptist* exercised the cy pres authority to designate successor takers on dissolution.[293] Under the "corporate autonomy" approach, the decisions of the corporate or church authorities within the framework of the corporate articles would be final on who should take on dissolution, so long as they did not direct the property outside the broadly defined limits of permissible charitable activities. The latter approach is clearly preferable in terms of minimizing official interference with ecclesiastical autonomy.

It is ironic that the implied trust theory, which originated in the resolution of church property disputes and which four California Court of Appeal decisions have now rejected for that purpose, seems to persist in California as a common-law basis for the regulation of churches.

The *Faith Center* case[294] relied on the implied trust theory as a basis for the attorney general's exercise of supervisory authority over church corporations and related entities. This subject has been decisively influenced by California legislation, both before and after the court's decision.

Effective January 1, 1980, the Corporations Code provisions on Nonprofit Corporations and Corporations for Charitable or Eleemosynary Purposes (including key sections 9505, 10206, and 10207) were repealed and replaced by a comprehensive new codification that established separate consolidated sections on Nonprofit Public Benefit, Nonprofit Mutual Benefit, and Nonprofit Religious Cor-

---

[293] Discussed in text accompanying note 272 *supra*.

[294] Younger v. Faith Center, Inc., Civ. No. 56574 (Cal. Ct. App. Aug. 29, 1980) (unpublished), discussed in text accompanying note 13 *supra*.

porations.[295] There are persuasive indications that the new codification of Nonprofit Religious Corporations[296] was intended to repeal the implied trust doctrine and limit the court's and the attorney general's supervisory powers to the authority specifically conferred by this legislation. The implied trust language from section 10206(c) was not reinstated in the new legislation.[297] In addition, the attorney general is not listed as one of the parties who can bring an action to remedy a breach involving a religious corporation,[298] a definite change from the prior law and a contrast to the provisions governing public benefit or mutual benefit corporations.[299] The standards of conduct for directors of religious corporations are also less stringent than for the other types of corporations.[300] These distinctions are said to have stemmed from concerns about the special First Amendment position of the religious corporation and from policy disagreement among the draftsmen on how much regulation should be imposed on the secular affairs of churches.[301]

Although the new Nonprofit Religious Corporations Code seriously limited official supervisory authority over religious corpora-

---

[295] Act of Aug. 29, 1978, ch. 567, 1978 Cal. Stats. 1740 (amended by Act of Sept. 14, 1979, ch. 681, 1979 Cal. Stat. 2130) (codified as CAL. CORP. CODE §§ 5110-6910, 7110-8910, 9110-9690 (West Supp. 1981). For an excellent history of this new legislation and its antecedents, see Abbott & Kornblum, *The Jurisdiction of the Attorney General Over Corporate Fiduciaries Under the New California Nonprofit Corporation Law*, 13 U.S.F.L. REV. 753 (1979). For a more critical analysis, see Toms & Runquist, *The Government's Role in the "Purification" of Religious Organizations*, 7 PEPPERDINE L. REV. 355 (1980); Note, note 11 *supra*.

[296] CAL. CORP. CODE § 9110-9160 (West Supp. 1981).

[297] *See* CAL. CORP. CODE §§ 5140, 9140 (West Supp. 1981). Section 10206(c) is quoted and discussed in text accompanying note 254 *supra*.

[298] CAL. CORP. CODE § 9142 (West Supp. 1981).

[299] *See* CAL. CORP. CODE §§ 5142, 7142 (West Supp. 1981); Abbott & Kornblum, *supra* note 295, at 789, 792.

[300] Abbott & Kornblum, *supra* note 295, at 793.

[301] *Id*. at 790.

tions, it did not eliminate it altogether, as did the California enactment of the Uniform Supervision of Trustees for Charitable Purposes Act, which exempted any "religious corporation or organization which holds property for religious purposes."[302] In section 9320 the new code gave the attorney general power, "upon reasonable ground to believe that the following condition or conditions have occurred or do exist," to examine a corporation to determine whether (1) it failed to qualify as a religious corporation; (2) there had been fraudulent activity in connection with corporate property; (3) such property had been diverted for personal benefit; (4) contributions solicited from the general public for specific corporate purposes had been diverted from their stated purpose; or (5) there had been substantial diversion of corporate assets from stated corporate purposes.[303]

The outcry caused by the attorney general's investigatory activities under the new Nonprofit Religious Corporations Code and his interpretations of prior law, such as in the *Faith Center* and *Worldwide Church of God* cases,[304] resulted in the repeal of section 9230 of the new code just nine months after it became effective. The repealing legislation seems calculated to eliminate any existing statutory or common-law basis for attorney general supervisory jurisdiction over church corporations other than the limited authority specifically enacted in the new bill. Thus, after citing federal and state constitutional guarantees of free exercise and nonestablishment, section one of the new legislation declares:

> Such protections and heritage require that government action regarding religious bodies must be narrow and minimal. The Legislature hereby declares that the power of the State of California with respect to the formation, existence, and operation of religious corporations shall be limited to those expressly provided in statutes duly enacted by this Legislature. . . . [305]

---

[302] Cal. Gov't Code § 12853 (West 1980), discussed in text accompanying note 262 *supra*.

[303] Cal. Corp. Code § 9230 (West Supp. 1981).

[304] *See* notes 11-16 and accompanying text *supra*.

[305] S.B. 1493 (known as the Petris Bill), 1980 Cal. Stats. ch. 1324, § 1.

Section 9230 is then reenacted to give the attorney general authority to challenge a religious corporation's qualification, to enforce or obtain restitution under the criminal laws, to assist state agencies in regulating activities in which religious corporations, along with other entities, are engaged, and to institute an action to enforce the "charitable trust" when property has been solicited and received from the general public on a representation that it would be used for a specific charitable purpose other than general corporate support and it is being diverted from such purpose.[306] The attorney general is forbidden from exercising any other powers "with respect to any corporation incorporated or classified as a religious corporation under or pursuant to this Code."[307] In view of this drastic reduction in the extent of supervisory authority that the attorney general had been exercising over religious charitable corporations under former section 9230 and the so-called "public trust doctrine," it is not surprising that the attorney general responded to the passage of this legislation by dismissing the *Faith Center* and *Worldwide Church of God* cases and the investigations described earlier.[308]

---

[306] CAL. CORP. CODE § 9230(b),(c) & (d) (West Supp. 1981) (amended by S.B. 1493, 1980 Cal. Stats. ch. 1324).

[307] CAL. CORP. CODE § 9230(a) (West Supp. 1981).

[308] *AG will Dismiss Cases Involving Religious Groups*, L.A. Daily J., Oct. 15, 1980; notes 13-16 and accompanying text *supra*.

VI

CONSTITUTIONAL
CONSIDERATIONS
AND CONCLUSION

A. REGULATORY AUTHORITY

As shown in Parts II and III, the attorney general had a clear common-law duty to invoke the inherent powers of a court of equity to *establish and defend* charitable trusts. As applied to churches or religious trusts, that enforcement power is not likely to impinge upon First Amendment rights, since it is supportive of the trust and the trustee. The attorney general's exercise of what this Article has called *responsible representation*[309] can likewise be supportive of the trust, but it can also pose threats to religious freedom if that officer attempts to substitute his judgment for the judgment of church authorities in replacing the trustees or remodeling the trust by cy pres. When applied to religious trusts or church corporations, the other two enforcement

---

[309] *See generally* text accompanying notes 140-50 *supra*.

functions, *investigation and supervision* and *challenging breaches of trusts*, are inevitably at odds with the free exercise and anti-establishment guarantees of the First Amendment to the United States Constitution.

Most of the examples of regulatory authority asserted over religious trusts or church corporations come from California in the last decade. In that state, the attorney general has asserted the common-law right to "supervise" church corporations and trusts for religious purposes on the basis that all such entities "are trustees of their assets for public benefit."[310] This theory, which has been called the "public trust doctrine," has been used by the California attorney general as the basis for the following actions, aimed at investigating or correcting alleged breaches of trust involving church properties (principally misappropriation for personal use or other diversion from religious use):

(1) taking over management of church properties and finances by appointment of a receiver;

(2) seeking to remove church officers and trustees and appoint successors;

(3) seeking accounting of funds received and disbursed by church officers and corporations;

(4) seeking discovery of numerous categories of financial, corporate, and personnel documents, including communications among church officials and ministers;[311] and

(5) replacing church decisions with his own recommendations for disposition of church assets by cy pres.[312]

Other attorneys general have asserted their common-law enforcement powers as a basis for investigating the activities and administration of public charities,[313] but in no other state has this investigatory power been applied to church corporations or to religious trusts.

---

[310] Respondent's Brief, *supra* note 16, at 16-17.

[311] *See* notes 10-15 and accompanying text *supra*.

[312] *See* Metropolitan Baptist Church of Richmond, Inc. v. Younger, 48 Cal. App. 3d 850, 121 Cal. Rptr. 899 (1975), discussed in text at note 272 *supra*.

[313] *See* cases discussed in text accompanying notes 150 & 152 *supra*.

As is evident from Parts II and III, claims to common-law authority for attorney general supervisory jurisdiction over religious charities are grossly overstated, if not altogether specious. Such authority is even withheld in all state statutes conferring supervisory jurdisdiction, as shown in part IV. Finally, Part V shows that California's public trust doctrine is descended not from the common law of judicial and attorney general enforcement authority over charitable trusts, but from a misapplication of the implied trust doctrine that the English and American courts evolved as a tool for resolving church property disputes. Born a naked legal fiction, the doctrine of implied trust had a robust role in church property disputes in this country for about a century but has now been consigned to oblivion as a dispute-settlement mechanism by 1969 and 1979 United States Supreme Court decisions, holding it unconstitutional.[314] With that illegitimate ancestry, California's unique court decisions and legislative enactments using the implied trust doctrine to justify judicial and attorney general supervision of religious charitites are at least seriously suspect on the same grounds. The California Court of Appeal decisions on church property disputes are taking these constitutional doubts seriously,[315] and the Legislature has responded to the excesses of the attorney general by rescinding the legislative basis for the public trust doctrine.[316].

The first section of this Part will discuss the validity of attorney general enforcement and the supervisory powers over religious trusts and corporations, measuring them against the religion clauses of the First Amendment. The treatment is necessarily illustrative rather than exhaustive.[317]

1. Free exercise

Because an assertion of judicial and attorney general supervisory jurisdiction over religious charitable trusts and corporations pro-

---

[314] Cases discussed in text accompanying notes 355-56 *infra*.

[315] Cases discussed in text at notes 284-87 *supra*.

[316] *See* text accompanying note 304 *supra*.

[317] *See generally* Note, note 11 *supra*; Weiss, *Privilege, Posture and Protection—"Religion" in the Law*, YALE L.J. 593 (1964); Toms & Runquist, note 295 *supra*; other authorities cited at note 11 *supra*.

vides a means of state surveillance, regulation, and control over the exercise of religious privileges, it is at least a presumptive violation of the guarantee of free exercise of religion. As practiced in California, where the attorney general has invoked equity powers to prevent religious charities from departing from the general purpose for which they were formed,[318] this supervision inevitably involves official authorities in monitoring and ruling upon religious doctrine and practice, since the purposes of a religious organization are, by definition, overtly religious in nature. Surveillance of churches and official consideration of religious matters are clearly forbidden by the First Amendment.[319]

The mechanisms of enforced disclosure incident to such surveillance and determination are also unconstitutional. As the American Civil Liberties Union of Southern California argued in one of the *Worldwide Church of God* cases:

> No single device is more evocative of inquisitorial power or susceptible to inquisitorial abuse than the power of coerced disclosure. Theoretical free exercise is of little moment if the private church organizations which give substance and effect to joint belief are subject to surveillance and control, their institutional records and papers may be seized, their leaders may be summoned to submit to public interrogation and to justify the manner in which they carry out their religious mission.[320]

The Supreme Court's earliest holding on this subject, that compelled disclosure of NAACP membership lists violated the First Amendment rights of free speech and free association,[321] was followed by a whole line of precedents the Supreme Court recently characterized as

---

[318] *See* text accompanying note 272-308 *supra*.

[319] Presbyterian Church v. Mary E. B. Hull Memorial Presbyterian Church, 393 U.S. 440 (1969); Surinach v. Pesquera de Busquets, 604 F.2d 73 (1st Cir. 1979).

[320] Brief of American Civil Liberties Union of Southern California *et al.* as Amici Curiae at 13-14, Worldwide Church of God, Inc. v. California, 449 U.S. 900 (1980) (denying cert.).

[321] NAACP v. Alabama, 357 U.S. 449, 462 (1958). *See also* Shelton v. Tucker, 364 U.S. 479 (1960).

standing for the proposition that compelled disclosure "cannot be justified by a mere showing of some legitimate governmental interest."[322] Instead, the proposed "subordinating interests of the State must survive exacting scrutiny."[323] This "strict test" is necessary, the Court said, "because compelled disclosure has the potential for substantially infringing the exercise of First Amendment rights."[324]

The regulatory facts in *Surinach v. Pesquera de Busquets*[325] are probably more analogous to the attorney general's supervisory jurisdiction over religious entities than those of any other federal appellate decision. In *Surinach* the Court of Appeals for the First Circuit enjoined the Puerto Rican Department of Consumer Affairs from compelling Catholic schools to disclose financial information the Department needed for its inflation-controlling investigation into the skyrocketing costs of private schools. In holding that this inquiry infringed religious freedom, the court stated:

> The Department's attempt to take its first steps down its regulatory road by gathering information accordingly are suspect, both in light of the purpose for which the information is sought and in itself, for as has long been recognized, "compelled disclosure has the potential for substantially infringing the exercise of First Amendment rights." *Buckley v. Valeo, supra*, 424 U.S. at 66, 96 S.Ct. at 657. We see that potential in the chilling of the decision making process, occasioned by the threat that those decisions will become the subject of public hearings and that eventually, if found wanting, will be supplanted by government control.[326]

A systematic monitoring of the financial affairs of churches almost certainly infringes the free exercise of religion. The more intrusive official interventions, such as the appointment of a receiver or the replacement of church officers, are even more obvious infringements of free exercise.

---

[322] Buckley v. Valeo, 424 U.S. 1, 64 (1976).

[323] *Id.*

[324] *Id.* at 66.

[325] 604 F.2d 73 (1st Cir. 1979).

[326] *Id.* at 78. *Accord*, Fernandes v. Limmer, 465 F. Supp. 493, 504-05 (N.D. Tex. 1979).

2. Establishment

As a means of institutionalizing a control relationship between state officials and religious institutions, the public trust doctrine was, in itself, a forbidden establishment of religion. The means by which the attorney general's supervisory jurisdiction was implemented—from the extreme remedy of receivership to the mere monitoring of activities—also constitute a forbidden official entanglement in church affairs. As Professor Laurence H. Tribe argued (as counsel) in one of the *Worldwide Church of God* appeals, "For the State, through its receiver, to run a church—even for the time it takes to prepare for and conduct a trial—*is* an 'establishment of religion' in its purest and most obvious form."[327] More generally, as the American Civil Liberties Union argued in an earlier proceeding: "If the common law transforms every California church into a public trust with the State as the ultimate trustee for the beneficiary public, then the State is the *ultimate* establishment."[328] In other words, controls exercised over churches or religious leaders should have to be justified under the police power, subject to the constraints of the First Amendment. But under the public trust doctrine the state asserts an enforcement position under charitable trust theory that gives it an additional source of power over religious organizations. That increment of power—more than the state enjoys over individuals or businesses—adds up to an establishment of religion.

This is essentially the same point noted by the New York Court of Appeals in 1854: If religious corporations hold their property in trust for the members and purposes of the church, this will inevitably involve the courts in the administration of the entire property of re-

---

[327] Appellant's Opening Brief at 94, People v. Worldwide Church of God, Inc., Civ. No. 57321 (Cal. Ct. App. June 30, 1980). Leo Pfeffer, attorney for amici curiae, called this "[t]he most flagrant violation of the mandate of the establishment clause," declaring that "[t]he very appointment of a receiver to manage and control the operation of a church reeks of excessive entanglement." Motion for Leave to File Brief Amici Curiae and Brief of National Council of Churches of Christ in the U.S.A., *et al.* at 20, Worldwide Church of God, Inc. v. California, 449 U.S. 900 (1980) (denying cert.). *Accord*, Worthing, *supra* note 11, at 146.

[328] Brief, *supra* note 320, at 15.

ligious corporations and in the interpretation of church doctrines.[329] This was also the result the United States Supreme Court sought to avoid by holding the implied trust doctrine unconstitutional in church property disputes.[330] It would be ironic if a doctrine that was impermissible as a basis for choosing between two contending factions in a dispute over church property could nevertheless be employed as a basis for granting an equity court and the attorney general continuing supervisory jurisdiction over the administration of that same property.

If the public trust doctrine is not an invalid establishment on its face, it must surely be so in its implementation. If churches and religious trusts are obliged to account to the attorney general, who is authorized to examine their affairs, supervise the management of their property, and regulate their activities, an institutionalized entanglement would seem to be inescapable.[331] Thus, in *Surinach v. Pesquera de Busquets*,[332] the court gave the church schools injunctive relief because the Department's financial oversight was a violation of the establishment clause:

> The subpoenas which generated this controversy sought extremely detailed information about the expenditure of funds of these Catholic schools. If the schools are forced to comply, that information will be subjected to governmental perusal, to public examination, and ultimately may form the basis for significant governmental involvement in their fiscal management. . . . This governmental program thus has the "self-perpetuating and self-expanding propensities" which have alerted courts to an increased danger of an unconstitutional degree of entanglement.

---

[329] Robertson v. Bullions, 11 N.Y. 243, 247 (1854), discussed in text accompanying note 185 *supra*.

[330] Presbyterian Church v. Mary E. B. Hull Memorial Presbyterian Church, 393 U.S. 440 (1969); Jones v. Wolf, 443 U.S. 595 (1979), discussed in text accompanying notes 355-56 *infra*.

[331] Brief, *supra* note 320, at 15-16. *Cf.* Walz v. Tax Comm'n, 397 U.S. 664, 676 (1970); Lemon v. Kurtzman, 403 U.S. 602 (1971); Levitt v. Committee for Pub. Educ. & Religious Liberty, 413 U.S. 472 (1973).

[332] 604 F.2d 73 (1st Cir. 1979).

... [T]his regulatory scheme ... does, however, permit it to intrude upon decisions of religious authorities as to how much money should be expended and how funds should best be allotted to serve the religious goals of the schools. [This] form of involvement strikes us as "a relationship pregnant with dangers of excessive governmental direction of church schools and hence of churches."[333]

What *Surinach* said of government financial supervision of church schools is, of course, even more true as to government supervision of churches. The fact that the apprehended dangers have not yet occurred is irrelevant. One of the significant functions of the establishment clause is to prohibit structural relationships under which abuses (such as interferences with the free exercise of religion) can occur. The whole theory of entanglement focuses on "potential" rather than proof of harm. The fact that there may have been no intent to regulate the ecclesiastical affairs of churches under the public trust doctrine or other supervisory effort is likewise insufficient, since probable effect, as well as intent, is a test of the validity of regulations of this nature.[334] The North Carolina Supreme Court used similar reasoning in holding that that state's Solicitation of Charita-

---

[333] *Id.* at 78, 79 (quoting Lemon v. Kurtzman, 403 U.S. 602, 620 (1971)). *Accord*, Heritage Village Church & Missionary Fellowship v. State, 299 N.C. 399, 263 S.E.2d 726 (1980):

As applied to religious organizations, the enforcement of these provisions inevitably entangles the state and its agencies in a persistent inquiry into whether particular expenditures of a religious organization are secular or religious in nature, or whether the religious expenditures support the same religious purposes represented in the organization's license application. . . .
. . . The potential exists for the state not only to substitute its own judgment as to the substantive "purpose" of a particular expenditure, but also to inject itself into the very center of religious disputes.

Id. at 735 (footnote omitted).

[334] "While we agree that there has been no showing of any purpose to inhibit religion, the effect of the Commonwealth's actions, even though aimed at private schools in general, constitutes a palpable threat of state interference with the internal policies and benefits of these church related schools." 604 F.2d at 76-77.

ble Funds Act could not be constitutionally applied to churches because of the danger of entanglement.[335]

These rulings clearly invalidate the use of the public trust theory and other efforts to acquire supervisory jurisdiction over church corporations and religious charitable trusts.

3. Compelling state interest and alternate means tests

The only way a governmental entity can validly take action that constitutes an infringement on the free exercise of religion is (1) to justify its action under some "compelling state interest" and (2) show that there are no less intrusive alternate means by which that interest can be vindicated.[336] The free exercise violation entailed in judicial and attorney general supervision of religious charities cannot pass either part of that test. There is no compelling state interest in such

---

[335] Heritage Village Church & Missionary Fellowship v. State, 299 N.C. 399, 263 S.E.2d 726 (1980):

> Absent narrow circumstances of outright fraud or collusion or other specific illegality, the propriety of a religious organization's expenditures can be evaluated only by reference to the organization's own doctrinal goals and procedures. The question of proper purpose is an ecclesiastical one, and its resolution necessarily entails an interpretive inquiry into possible deviations from religious policy. "But this is exactly the inquiry that the First Amendment prohibits. ..." Serbian Orthodox Diocese v. Milivojevich, 426 U.S. 696, 713 (1976).
> ...
> We do not intend to intimate that the state will seek to apply the Act's provisions to religious organizations in such a way as to dictate the bounds of religious purpose. But the potential for such abuse is clear when the factors discussed above are considered cumulatively. We find that the Act, as applied to plaintiff religious organizations, is characterized by excessive entanglements between the state and religion and poses significant risks of secular interference with rights of conscience.

299 N.C. at 415-16, 263 S.E.2d at 735-36 (citations omitted).

[336] Thomas v. Review Bd., 450 U.S. 707, 715 (1981); Sherbert v. Verner, 374 U.S. 398, 403, 406 (1963); Wisconsin v. Yoder, 406 U.S. 205, 229-30 (1972); People v. Woody, 61 Cal. 2d 716, 394 P.2d 813, 40 Cal. Rptr. 69 (1964); L. TRIBE, AMERICAN CONSTITUTIONAL LAW 846-59 (1978).

supervision, and there are less intrusive alternate means to vindicate the state's interest in this area.

Despite the important public interest in the inflation-controlling efforts of the Department in the *Surinach* case, the departmental orders that the church schools produce financial information were invalidated by the court of appeals because the department was unable to show that those interests "[rose] to the level of those which have been found to outweigh First Amendment religious freedoms."[337] Other cases which have applied the rule that the state cannot infringe upon religious freedom without meeting the stringent compelling state interest test underline the vitality of this requirement.[338]

What is the compelling state interest in investigating, supervising, and correcting breaches of trust in religious charitable trusts and corporations? What kinds of breaches are likely to occur in the context of churches or religious trusts? The studies that led to the passage of the Uniform Supervision of Trustees for Charitable Purposes Act disclosed very little dishonest administration of charitable trusts generally and apparently reported no concerns whatever with religious organizations. As to charitable trustees generally, they reported six principal types of abuses: (1) unwise investments, (2) vacancies in the trusteeship, (3) need to remodel the trust instrument under cy pres because of changed conditions, (4) dormancy of the trust or lack of initiative by the trustee, (5) danger of reversion for noncompliance with conditions of the gift, and (6) excessive compensation to the

---

[337] 604 F.2d at 80. *See also* Tribe, *Foreword: Toward a Model of Roles in the Due Process of Life and Law*, 87 HARV. L. REV. 1, 22-26 (1973) (arguing for a similar test in the establishment area).

[338] *E.g.*, Edwards v. Maryland State Fair & Agricultural Soc'y, Inc., 628 F.2d 282 (4th Cir. 1980); International Soc'y for Krishna Consciousness, Inc. v. Bowen, 600 F.2d 667, 669 (7th Cir. 1979); United States v. Boesewetter, 463 F. Supp. 370 (D.D.C. 1978): Iskon v. Hays, 438 F. Supp. 1077 (S.D. Fla. 1977); *cf.* Heffron v. International Soc'y for Krishna Consciousness, 101 S. Ct. 2559 (1981) (time, place, and manner restrictions on distribution of religious literature at state fair must be justified by a "significant governmental interest" and must leave open ample alternative channels to communicate the information).

trustee.[339] None of these seems of significant public concern with respect to churches or religious charitable trusts. While there may be cases of such abuses by trustees holding for the benefit of churches, the church's own rights of enforcement of the trust—sufficient in some cases even to deny the attorney general any enforcement role as a matter of law—[340]seem at least sufficient to prevent the state from having any "compelling state interest" in the enforcement of religious charitable trusts for the benefit of organized churches or their purposes.

As for incorporated charities, including incorporated churches, the significant alternative enforcement mechanisms that could be used for charitable corporations (which justified the common-law restrictions on judicial and attorney general enforcement of this form of charity[341]) make this an even clearer case for the absence of a compelling state interest. For example, church members' self interest moves them to watch their leaders' performances, and they can exercise significant corrective control by the power of the purse. Unlike the traditional charitable trust, which involved the administration of an endowed fund contributed in the past, a church is generally dependent upon a continued flow of contributions from its members. The confidence of church membership is therefore an essential ingredient for church officers and trustees. If the membership, or any individual member, is dissatisfied with the decisions of its leaders or even with their nondisclosure or inaccessibility to questions about financial matters, they can withhold further contributions and other patronage. That is the ultimate membership control over churches. On the other hand, as to funds already contributed without any express trust or restriction, the rule should be, as has been held:

> [B]y his act of donating his money he manifests his decision to entrust the control and disposition of his funds to the Church and those who manage it. And the donor has no right to retrieve, control, or direct the manner in which the money so given shall be used simply because

---

[339] Bogert, *supra* note 207, at 635-36, 643; Note, *State Supervision of the Administration of Charitable Trusts*, 47 COLUM. L. REV. 659, 660-61 (1947).

[340] *See* text accompanying note 154 *supra*.

[341] *See* text accompanying notes 161-92 *supra*.

he has made such contributions to the Church, nor because he is a member of the class which may be benefited by the carrying out of its purposes.[342]

This ruling that a contributor has no enforceable interest in an unrestricted donation to a church—the antithesis of the discredited implied trust doctrine—should foster the kind of "hands off churches" approach that is consistent with churches' special position under the First Amendment.[343]

The state is also obliged, as the court of appeals concluded in *Surinach*, "to show cause that it has pursued its secular objectives in the manner which is least intrusive upon religious concerns."[344] The fact that there are alternative, less intrusive means available to vindicate the state's interests negates the existence of a compelling state interest and shows that the attorney general's attempted supervision of religious entities by the public trust doctrine also fails under the alternate means test.

An important avowed purpose of the public trust doctrine in California was to prevent fraud under the guise of religion.[345] But the

---

[342] Stone v. Salt Lake City, 11 Utah 2d 196, 201, 356 P.2d 631, 634 (1960).

[343] Compare this ruling with CAL. CORP. CODE §§ 9511, 9512, 9514, 9243(c)(1), 9243(h) (West Supp. 1981), which give members of nonprofit religious corporations rights of inspection of corporate membership and financial records and causes of action for accounting and damages to remedy self-dealing transactions. The constitutionality of this new legislation has yet to be determined.

[344] 604 F.2d at 80. *Accord*, that this an an additional requirement, cases cited at note 338 *supra. Cf.* Village of Schaumburg v. Citizens for Better Environment, 444 U.S. 620 (1980) (city's legitimate interest in preventing fraud can be better served by measures less intrusive on First Amendment freedoms than a direct prohibition on charitable solicitation.)

[345] *See* text accompanying notes 12-16 *supra*. In the month following repeal of that doctrine by statute, the California attorney general complained to the legislature that the repealing legislation had removed "all of the Attorney General's pre-existing powers to investigate and bring action for internal fiscal (civil) fraud in connection with religious corporations," citing as examples his inability to "bring actions against individual directors and agents of religious corporations for self-dealing, breach of trust, and diversion of assets contrary to corporate purposes." California Attorney General, Memorandum to Assembly Judiciary Committee on Interim Hearings on Senate Bill 1493 (Petris), November 12, 1980, at 1.

state is by no means without legal remedies against such frauds. The criminal law is, or can be made to be, adequate to the task of suppressing fraud and other criminal conduct committed by religious leaders, churches, or associated trusts or corporations. Thus, the United States Supreme Court has repeatedly declared that if persons commit fraud upon the public under the mantle of religion, "penal laws are available to punish such conduct,"[346] and there are illustrations of the application of that principle by lower courts.[347] The existence of a compelling state interest to prevent crimes in the name of religion is not subject to doubt.[348] These alternative means, using the police power and the civil remedies summarized below, are preferable to the public trust doctrine because they involve no new theory of power over churches and they minimize forbidden official entanglements with churches.

Equitable remedies like the injunction or the constructive trust are also available to correct civil wrongs committed in the name of religion.[349] Laws designed to regulate businesses apply to the busi-

---

[346] Cantwell v. Connecticut, 310 U.S. 296, 306 (1940) (dictum); Schneider v. New Jersey, 308 U.S. 147, 164 (1939) (dictum); United States v. Ballard, 322 U.S. 78, 95 (1944) (dictum) (Jackson, J. dissenting). *Accord*, Karst, *supra* note 211 at 464. *Cf.* Prince v. Massachusetts, 321 U.S. 158 (1944) (religious duty no defense to criminal prosecution for permitting minor to distribute religious literature in violation of child labor law); Branzburg v. Hayes, 408 U.S. 665, 691 (1972) (though involved with essential First Amendment activity, news gathering is not immune from requirements of criminal law).

[347] SEC v. World Radio Mission, Inc., 544 F.2d 535 (1st Cir. 1976); People v. Estep, 346 Ill. App. 132, 104 N.E.2d 562 (1952); Chedester v. State, 91 Nev. 316, 535 P.2d 794 (1975); People v. LeGrande, 309 N.Y. 420, 131 N.E.2d 712 (1956).

[348] United States v. Kuch, 288 F. Supp. 439 (D.D.C. 1968); Lawson v. Commonwealth, 291 Ky. 437, 164 S.W.2d 972 (1942); People v. Strong, 45 A.D.2d 18, 356 N.Y.S.2d 200 (1974); State v. Bullard, 267 N.C. 599, 148 S.E.2d 565 (1966); Harden v. State, 188 Tenn. 17, 216 N.W.2d 708 (1949); cases cited at notes 346 & 347 *supra*.

[349] *E.g.*, Barber v. Irving, 226 Cal. App. 2d 560, 38 Cal. Rptr. 142 (1964); Scott v. Thompson, 21 Iowa 599 (1866); Latham v. Father Divine, 299 N.Y. 22, 85 N.E.2d 168 (1949); Seventh Elect Church in Israel v. First Seattle Dexter Horton Nat'l Bank, 162 Wash. 437, 299 P. 359 (1931).

ness activities of churches,[350] although there are special religious immunities that must be considered when commercial activities are intimately intertwined with (rather than merely a revenue source for) the religious mission of churches. The content and administration of the federal tax laws provides sufficient and perhaps even excessive oversight over the financial and licensed commercial activities of churches.[351] Finally, the traditional remedy of quo warranto can serve as an effective, but appropriately restrained, ultimate sanction against religious corporations that exceed or abuse their charter powers.[352]

The attorney general's traditional concern with enforcing charitable trusts for the good of the public applies with far less force to the church or religious charitable corporation or trust, for the reasons discussed earlier.[353] And with churches or other religious organizations, there are vital and countervailing constitutional rights that mandate minimum official intervention. As a result, the risk that some trustees or corporate officers would commit breaches of trust to the detriment of their members does not seem to entail the kind of compelling state interest that would override the risk that the official

---

[350] *E.g.*, SEC v. World Radio Mission, Inc., 544 F.2d 535 (1st Cir. 1976) (enjoining religious organizations' misrepresentations in security offerings); Muhammad Temple of Islam-Shreveport v. City of Shreveport, 387 F. Supp. 1129 (W.D. La. 1974), *aff'd on opinion below*, 517 F.2d 922 (5th Cir. 1975) (sale of foodstuffs); Moritz v. United Brethrens Church on Staten Island, 269 N.Y. 125, 199 N.E. 29 (1935) (use of church land for burial purposes).

[351] *E.g.*, Christian Echoes National Ministry, Inc. v. United States, 470 F.2d 849 (10th Cir. 1972) (revocation of federal tax exemption for excessive attempts to influence legislation), *discussed in* Borod, *Lobbying for the Public Interest—Federal Tax Policy and Administration*, 42 N.Y.U. L. REV. 1087 (1967); Rev. Rul. 78-385, 1978-2 C.B. 174 (amplifying Rev. Rul. 68-563, 1968-2 C.B. 212 (unrelated business income from church-operated television station)); I.R.S. Letter Ruling 7838036 (unrelated business income from monastery's production of food items and sale of nonreligious items in gift shop); Karst, *supra* note 211 at 437-43 ("indirect enforcement" of charitable trusts by tax officials).

[352] Discussed in text accompanying notes 173-77 *supra*.

[353] *See* text accompanying notes 161-205 & 345-52 *supra*.

mechanisms formed to deal with possible breaches could be adapted to purposes destructive of religious freedom. This was undoubtedly the judgment of the state legislatures which have, to date, enacted comprehensive charitable trust enforcement legislation in fifteen states. In all fifteen states, the legislatures have exempted religious charitable trusts and corporations from the enforcement powers conferred on the courts and the attorney general.[354] That is a persuasive national verdict on the absence of a compelling state interest in the public trust doctrine or other statutory or common-law rules for supervising religious charitable trusts or corporations.

In order to minimize official involvement in the interpretation and administration of religious charitable trusts and corporations, courts construing the terms of gifts to religious organizations should exercise a strong preference for finding gifts absolute rather than in trust, unrestricted rather than restricted. A clear and convincing evidence test should be required to establish a trust obligation or an enforceable restriction in connection with such a gift. And when remedies against religious organizations can be justified, the court should always prefer a negative and one-time remedy like injunction of quo warranto over an entangling positive remedy that entails continuing official oversight like the public trust doctrine.

B. CHURCH PROPERTY DISPUTES

The relevance of trust doctrines to church property disputes did not cease when the United States Supreme Court rejected a century of state-court precedents and invalidated the implied trust doctrine on constitutional grounds in *Presbyterian Church v. Mary E.B. Hull Memorial Presbyterian Church*[355] and in *Jones v. Wolf*.[356] The substitu-

---

[354] Discussed in text accompanying note 227 *supra*.

[355] 393 U.S. 440 (1969), *discussed in* Kauper, note 85 *supra*. Earlier church property decisions are discussed in Kauper, note 85 *supra*; Comment, note 85 *supra*; Note, note 85 *supra*. BYU law student Jeanne Bryan Inouye gave particularly valuable assistance in the analysis employed in this section.

[356] 443 U.S. 595 (1979), *discussed in* Comment, Jones v. Wolf: *Neutral Principles Standard of Review for Intra-Church Disputes*, 13 LOY. L.A.L. REV. 109 (1979) [hereinafter cited as Comment, Jones v. Wolf]; Comment, *Church Property Disputes: The Trend and the Alternative*, 31 MERCER L. REV. 559 (1980) [hereinafter cited as Comment, *Church Property Disputes*].

tion of an alternate theory like "neutral principles" will necessitate many years of litigation in the state and federal courts to define this new constitutional concept and to outline the parameters of its use. Trust doctrines are certain to continue to play a prominent role in future constitutional adjudication of church property disputes, since the *Hull* and *Jones* cases rejected the *implied* trust, not the *express* trust. The argument that one church body or officer holds property on an express trust for another church body remains viable.[357] This Article will therefore conclude with an examination of the constitutional doctrines that motivated the *Hull* and *Jones* decisions and a consideration of their application to the construction and enforcement of express trusts in church property disputes.

Both *Hull* and *Jones* involved Georgia judgments resolving property disputes growing out of schisms in the hierarchical Presbyterian Church in the United States. In both cases the state court had ruled in favor of the secessionist local congregation, and in both cases the United States Supreme Court reversed or vacated the judgment and remanded for further proceedings.

In *Hull* two local congregations, charging the hierarchy with departing from the tenets of faith held at the time of their affiliation (such as by the ordination of women ministers), withdrew from the general church organization. In a property contest the local churches prevailed in the state courts upon a jury finding that the general church had departed from a fundamental doctrine, thus forfeiting its interest in the local property, which was found to be held upon an implied trust for the general church on condition of adherence to doctrine. Writing for a unanimous Supreme Court, Justice Brennan reversed on the basis that the civil courts would have "*no* role in determining ecclesiastical questions in the process of resolving property disputes."[358] The departure-from-doctrine element of the implied trust theory was offensive because it required the courts to determine whether the challenged actions constituted a departure

---

[357] For an excellent illustration of the use of express trust theory in the resolution of a church property dispute, see Protestant Episcopal Church v. Barker, 115 Cal. App. 3d 599, 171 Cal. Rptr. 541 (1981).

[358] 393 U.S. at 447.

from doctrine and, if so, whether it was sufficiently important to the traditional theology to require that the trust be terminated. In the most frequently cited passage of its opinion, the Court said:

> Thus, the First Amendment severely circumscribes the role that civil courts may play in resolving church property disputes. It is obvious, however, that not every civil court decision as to property claimed by a religious organization jeopardizes values protected by the First Amendment. Civil courts do not inhibit free exercise of religion merely by opening their doors to disputes involving church property. And there are neutral principles of law, developed for use in all property disputes, which can be applied without "establishing" churches to which property is awarded. But First Amendment values are plainly jeopardized when church property litigation is made to turn on the resolution by civil courts of controversies over religious doctrine and practice. If civil courts undertake to resolve such controversies in order to adjudicate the property dispute, the hazards are ever present of inhibiting the free development of religious doctrine and of implicating secular interests in matters of purely ecclesiastical concern. Because of these hazards, the First Amendment enjoins the employment of organs of government for essentially religious purposes, *Abington School Dist. V. Schempp*, 374 U.S. 203 (1963); the Amendment therefore commands civil courts to decide church property disputes without resolving underlying controversies over religious doctrine.[359]

In *Jones* the majority of a local congregation voted to separate from the general church, but a minority opposed and its position and property ownership were sustained by an adjudicative body of the general church. Purporting to apply "neutral principles," the state courts relied on the fact that title was in the local congregation without any language of express trust in favor of the general church, and then ruled without explanation that the local congregation was represented by its majority faction. Because the state action did not reveal whether it was based on the permissible "neutral principle" of presumptive majority rule in congregational government [360] or upon an impermissible judicial consideration of church doctrine and policy as part of a conclusion that this result was dictated by church

---

[359] *Id.* at 449.

[360] 443 U.S. at 607.

law,[361] the Supreme Court vacated the judgment and remanded for the state court to articulate its basis for judgment. Discussing the "neutral principles of law" approach, which the Court said was "consistent with . . . constitutional principles," including the fact that the state could "adopt *any* one of various approaches for settling church property disputes so long as it involves no consideration of doctrinal matters,"[362] the Court stated the following:

> The neutral-principles approach was approved in *Maryland & Va. Churches*, supra, an appeal from a judgment of the Court of Appeals of Maryland settling a local church property dispute on the basis of the language of the deeds, the terms of the local church charters, the state statutes governing the holding of church property, and the provisions in the constitution of the general church concerning the ownership and control of church property. Finding that this analysis entailed "no inquiry into religious doctrine," the Court dismissed the appeal for want of a substantial federal question. 396 U.S., at 368.

> The primary advantages of the neutral-principles approach are that it is completely secular in operation, and yet flexible enough to accommodate all forms of religious organization and polity. The method relies exclusively on objective, well-established concepts of trust and property law familiar to lawyers and judges. It thereby promises to free civil courts completely from entanglement in questions of religious doctrine, polity, and practice. Furthermore, the neutral-principles analysis shares the peculiar genius of private-law systems in general—flexibility in ordering private rights and obligations to reflect the intentions of the parties.[363]

The Court then conceded that the neutral-principles approach was not wholly free from difficulty. In fact, it would require some examination of religious documents and perhaps some deferring to ecclesiastical decisions on the meaning of religious concepts:

> The neutral-principles method, at least as it has evolved in Georgia, requires a civil court to examine certain religious documents, such

---

[361] *Id*. at 609.

[362] *Id*. at 602-03 (quoting Maryland & Va. Eldership of the Churches of God v. Church of God at Sharpsburg, Inc., 396 U.S. 367, 368 (1970) (Brennan, J., concurring)) (emphasis in the original).

[363] 443 U.S. at 603.

as a church constitution, for language of trust in favor of the general church. In undertaking such an examination, a civil court must take special care to scrutinize the document in purely secular terms, and not to rely on religious precepts in determining whether the document indicates that the parties have intended to create a trust. In addition, there may be cases where the deed, the corporate charter, or the constitution of the general church incorporates religious concepts in the provisions relating to the ownership of property. If in such a case the interpretation of the instruments of ownership would require the civil court to resolve a religious controversy, then the court must defer to the resolution of the doctrinal issue by the authoritative ecclesiastical body. *Serbian Orthodox Diocese*, 426 U.S., at 709.

On balance, however, the promise of nonentanglement and neutrality inherent in the neutral-principles approach more than compensates for what will be occasional problems in application.[364]

The opinions of the Court in these two leading cases—unanimous in *Hull* and a five-justice majority in *Jones*—obviously represent a consensus of different groups of justices acting on quite different legal theories. Although coinciding for purposes of the result and opinion in these cases, these different theories will dictate different results in different factual situations, as is evident from studying concurring and dissenting opinions in all of the cases where the Supreme Court has applied the *Hull* principle. The three different theories will now be examined.

1. Three theories of the neutral-principles approach

a. Nondetermination of religious law or polity. For Justices Brennan (author of the *Hull* opinion), Douglas and Marshall, the critical passages in the *Hull* opinion were those that forbade civil courts from deciding church property disputes on the basis of their resolution of controversies over religious doctrine or practice. In a subsequent concurring opinion these three justices quoted those passages and added that their principle also forbade inquiries into church polity or to determine "whether the relevant church governing body has power under religious law to control the property in question."[365]

---

[364] *Id.* at 604.

[365] Maryland & Va. Eldership of the Churches of God v. Church of God at Sharpsburg, Inc., 396 U.S. 367, 369 (1970) (Brennan, J., concurring).

Courts could adopt any one of various approaches for settling church property disputes, including (1) the formal title doctrine, in which ownership is determined by studying deeds and general corporate laws, (2) special statutes, providing they left the court no role in determining ecclesiastical doctrine or polity, or (3) deferring to and enforcing the property decisions of church congregations or hierarchies, as prescribed in the *Watson* case, except that this would not be permissible where there was a "substantial controversy" over the identity of the church bodies that had authority to resolve the ownership of property under church law.[366] Under this approach, the justices declared (in words that cast doubt on the validity of express trusts premised upon religious conditions), any provision in a deed or other legal instrument whose enforcement required the court to resolve doctrinal questions or make an extensive inquiry into religious polity would be unenforceable in the civil courts.[367] Justice Blackmun, who came to the Court after the case was decided, probably subscribed to this view also.[368]

b. Neutrality in religious decision making. At the opposite extreme on the question of judicial involvement in questions of doctrine of polity are Justices Rehnquist and Stevens. For them the ruling principle in such cases is the establishment clause requirement of judicial neutrality among various religious beliefs, doctrines, or denominations

----

[366] *Id.* at 367-70.

[367] "Only express conditions that may be effected without consideration of doctrine are civilly enforceable." *Id.* at 369 n.2. "For example, provisions in deeds ... for the reversion of local church property to the general church, if conditioned upon a finding of departure from doctrine, could not be civilly enforced." *Id.* at 370. These passages seem to be a direct response to and contradiction of Justice Harlan's earlier suggestion that courts could decree a donor recovery of contributed property for the nonfulfillment of a condition premised upon religious doctrine. Presbyterian Church v. Mary E. B. Hull Memorial Presbyterian Church, 393 U.S. 440, 452 (1969) (Harlan, J., concurring).

[368] This inference is drawn from the fact that Justice Blackmun did not join the dissents in *Serbian* or *Jones*, discussed in text accompanying notes 369 & 375 *infra*, and did join the substantial incorporation of the *Sharpsburg* concurring opinion in the majority opinion in *Serbian*, 426 U.S. at 708-09.

and as between churches and other voluntary associations. In a case in which two factions in a hierarchical church contended for church office and property, a majority of the United States Supreme Court held that a state court could not review and set aside an ecclesiastical tribunal's decision for "arbitrariness" in failing to follow the church's own organic law and procedures.[369] In dissent, these two justices argued that there was no constitutional infirmity in a state court's attempting to determine which claimant was entitled to the church office (and thus to the property) "by application of the canon law of the church, just as they would have attempted to decide a similar dispute among the members of any other voluntary association."[370] The First Amendment requires that the government avoid "placing its weight behind a particular religious belief, tenet, or sect."[371] In addition to requiring that the state courts "remain neutral on matters of religious doctrine,"[372] this principle of neutrality also required that the courts not pursue noninvolvement in doctrine or polity to the point that they were giving "blind deference" to whatever they were told about church law or decisions by the "announced representatives" of a denomination:

> To make available the coercive powers of civil courts to rubber-stamp ecclesiastical decisions of hierarchical religious associations, when such deference is not accorded similar acts of secular voluntary associations, would, in avoiding the free exercise problems petitioners envision, itself create far more serious problems under the Establishment Clause.[373]

This approach of course minimizes any potential problems in the en-

---

[369] Serbian Orthodox Diocese v. Milivojevich, 426 U.S. 696 (1976).

[370] 426 U.S. at 726 (Rehnquist, J., dissenting).

[371] Id. at 733.

[372] Id. at 735.

[373] Id. at 734. For sharply differing points of view on whether the decisions of church bodies should be subject to the same or different judicial review than the decisions of other voluntary associations, see Kauper, *supra* note 85, at 373, 375; Note, *supra* note 85, at 1184-85; Comment, *supra* note 85, at 1136-38.

forcement or construction of express trusts or other deed provisions turning on the meaning of religious doctrine or polity.

c. Deference to church decisionmakers. The third group—Chief Justice Burger and Justices Stewart, White, and Powell—focus on free exercise rather than establishment. Their position was defined in their dissent, authored by Justice Powell, in *Jones v. Wolf*,[374] in which the majority upheld the state court's use of "neutral principles of law" even if this involved a different property disposition than that specified by an authoritative tribunal of a hierarchical church.[375] Pointing out the distorting effect of the "purely secular" reading of religious deeds and documents specified in the majority's opinion, the dissenters argued that the majority had violated free exercise rights by reversing the hierarchical organization established by church doctrine and practice and imposing a congregational polity on the church to resolve the property dispute in this case.[376] "This indirect interference by the civil court with the resolution of religious disputes within the church is no less proscribed by the First Amendment than is the direct decision of questions of doctrine and practice."[377] The key concept for these dissenters was compulsory deference to the decisions of church tribunals:

> Disputes among church members over the control of church property arise almost invariably out of disagreements regarding doctrine and practice. Because of the religious nature of these disputes, civil courts should decide them according to principles that do not interfere with the free exercise of religion in accordance with church polity and doctrine. . . . The only course that achieves this constitutional requirement is acceptance by civil courts of the decisions reached within the polity chosen by the church members themselves. The classic statement of this view is found in Watson v. Jones, 13 Wall., at 728-729. . .
>
> Accordingly, in each case involving an intrachurch dispute—including disputes over church property—the civil court must focus directly on ascertaining, and then following, the decision made

---

[374] 443 U.S. 595 (1979).

[375] *Id.* at 604.

[376] *Id.* at 612-13 (Powell, J., dissenting).

[377] *Id.* at 613.

within the structure of church governance. By doing so, the court avoids two equally unacceptable departures from the genuine neutrality mandated by the First Amendment. First, it refrains from direct review and revision of decisions of the church on matters of religious doctrines and practice that underlie the church's determination of intrachurch controversies, including those that relate to control of church property. Equally important . . . the civil court avoids interfering directly with the religious governance of those who have formed the association and submitted themselves to its authority.[378]

2. Future application of the neutral-principles approach

Since there is no clear majority for any of the three conceptual approaches described above, future cases are likely to be decided on the basis of coalitions of theories appropriate to the facts of the individual cases. For example, in *Serbian Orthodox Diocese v. Milivojevich*,[379] in which the state court was reversed for reviewing church law and rejecting the determination of the church tribunal, the majority was composed of the justices who espoused nondetermination of doctrine and those who espoused deference to the determination of church tribunals. Out of this coalition came the majority suggestion that "where resolution of the disputes cannot be made without extensive inquiry by civil courts into religious law and polity," the courts must accept "the decisions of the highest ecclesiastical tribunal within a church of hierarchical polity . . . as binding on them, in their application to the religious issues of doctrine or polity before them."[380] In this majority opinion the nondetermination/deference coalition also adopted Justice Brennan's concurring language from *Maryland & Virginia Eldership of the Churches of God v. Church of God at Sharpsburg*,

---

[378] *Id*. at 616-18 (citations omitted). This analysis is endorsed and elaborated on in Comment, Jones v. Wolf, note 356 *supra*; Comment, *Church Property Disputes*, note 356 *supra*.

[379] 426 U.S. 696 (1976).

[380] *Id*. at 709. In Jones v. Wolf, 443 U.S. 595, 604 (1979), the majority declared that in cases where the deed, corporate charter, or constitution "incorporates religious concepts in the provisions relating to the ownership of property," so that the civil courts must resolve a religious controversy in order to interpret them, "the court must defer to the resolution of the doctrinal issue by the authoritative ecclesiastical body."

Inc.[381] to the effect that the civil courts could not inquire into whether the relevant hierarchical church governing body has the power under church law to decide the property dispute.[382] One group apparently rejected this inquiry because of the illegitimacy of the court's review of church polity, and the other because of the court's failure to refer to the church tribunal.

Jones involved a different coalition. In *Jones* the nondetermination group joined the neutrality group. Though at odds on their willingness to have the court examine religious law (a matter not involved on the facts of this case), these two groups could join in a coalition to reject the compulsory deference to church tribunals proposed by the deference group in dissent. The nondeterminationists obviously rejected this approach because it would require the court "to examine the polity and administration of a church to determine which unit of government has ultimate control over church property."[383] The neutralists apparently rejected it because of the allure of "neutral principles" and because compulsory deference to religious tribunals and not to others would offend the principle of neutrality between churches and other voluntary associations. The price of this coalition was the nondeterminationists' acceptance of the validity of an express trust whose terms were predicated upon religious doctrine or polity, notwithstanding the fact that its enforcement or construction would require the civil courts to conduct some inquiry on these forbidden subjects.[384] How that procedure will be worked out in practice remains to be seen.

Other coalitions may evolve. For example, if a court's involvement in religious determinations incident to enforcing an express

---

[381] 396 U.S. 367 (1970).

[382] *Id.* at 369 (Brennan, J., concurring), *followed* in Serbian Orthodox Diocese v. Milivojevich, 426 U.S. 696, 708-09 (1976).

[383] Jones v. Wolf, 443 U.S. 595, 605 (1979).

[384] *Id.* at 600-01, 603, 604, 606, 608. The validity of an express trust that could only be enforced by some judicial inquiry into religious doctrine or polity was an open question after the *Hull* case, Kauper, *supra* note 85, at 369 n.73, and would have been precluded by the theory of the nondeterminationists. *See* text accompanying note 367 *supra*.

trust is too excessive for the nondeterminationists to accept, we may see a new coalition—the only combination as yet untried—between deference and neutrality. In this coalition a court could make a sufficient inquiry into church doctrine and practice to identify the appropriate tribunal to resolve an issue authoritatively under church law (something unacceptable to the nondeterminationists) and then apply that determination in some way sufficiently evenhanded by comparison to the review of other private associations so as to be acceptable to the neutralists. This coalition could also arise in a conflict over succession to leadership (and thus to control over property) in a hierarchical church. When that type of controversy arose in the *Serbian* case, it was resolved by a coalition of deference and nondetermination. It would require but little change in the facts or the Court's approach to them for this same controversy to be resolved by a coalition of deference and neutrality. Those who would defer to the church tribunal could do so on terms sufficiently evenhanded as to other private associations (including some inquiry into the authority of the church decisional body and the regularity of its proceedings) to satisfy those who seek neutrality. Whether this speculation is well founded or not, it identifies the kind of uncertainty inherent in future church property litigation that is subject to constitutional oversight from a United States Supreme Court which is, at this writing, divided 3-2-4 on the constitutional theory to be used in delineating what a civil court can and cannot do in resolving church property disputes.[385]

The type of coalition that unites to produce a majority resolution of church property disputes in the United States Supreme Court is

---

[385] Those counseling churches must at least assume that *Jones v. Wolf* has shifted the burden of protecting the property of hierarchical churches from the courts to the churches themselves. So long as there is no assured judicial deference to the decisions of ecclesiastical bodies (the position of the majority in *Jones*), hierarchical churches need to employ trust instruments or other deed or contract provisions to secure their ownership and control over church property being used by and titled in local congregations. It would also be prudent in drafting such provisions to hold the use of religious vocabulary and the involvement of religious doctrine to an absolute minimum.

also important because different coalitions incorporate different biases.

The deference/neutrality coalition is inherently biased in favor of a hierarchical body in any controversy with a secessionist congregation, since the hierarchy generally includes the tribunal to whose decision the courts gave deference. This is the bias inherent in *Watson v. Jones*,[386] whose general thrust was subordination to churches in property disputes. *Watson* would keep the courts out of religious *disputes*, even if it had to make some threshold decisions on religious doctrine and polity in order to identify the church authority to which it would defer.

The nondetermination/neutrality coalition is inherently biased in favor of a congregational group in any controversy with a hierarchical body, since the nondetermination requirement precludes the judicial inquiry necessary to authenticate the hierarchical tribunal or directive and thus forces the controversy to be resolved in terms of secular documents and principles.[387] This is the bias inherent in *Jones v. Wolf*,[388] whose general thrust was secularization of the resolution of church property disputes. *Jones* would keep the courts out of religious *doctrine*, even if that meant inhibiting the freedom of hierarchical churches to govern their internal affairs. The tensions inherent in these diverse emphases are likely to continue—with resulting uncertainties of outcome in litigated cases—until a majority of the Supreme Court espouses a single doctrinal approach to the resolution of church property controversies.

After a century of influence in church property controversies, the fictional implied trust doctrine is dead. The express trust remains viable, but the reluctance of some Supreme Court justices to have courts adjudicate any questions of religious doctrine or practice casts doubt over the utility of an express trust whose enforcement turns on such determinations. Finally, California's public trust doctrine, un-

---

[386] 80 U.S. (13 Wall.) 679 (1871), discussed in text accompanying note 98 *supra*.

[387] *See generally* Comment, Jones v. Wolf, note 356 *supra*; Comment, *Church Property Disputes*, note 356 *supra*.

[388] 443 U.S. 595 (1979).

der which the attorney general and the courts asserted the right to supervise religious charitable trusts and corporations, has recently been repealed, and was, in any case, unsupported by the common law and unconstitutional under the First Amendment.